the standard catalog of®

JOHN DEERE
TRACTORS

by Robert N. Pripps
Photography by Andrew Morland

©2004 Robert N. Pripps
Andrew Morland

Published by

kp books
An imprint of F+W Publications, Inc.

700 East State Street • Iola, WI 54990-0001
715-445-2214 • 888-457-2873

Our toll-free number to place an order or obtain
a free catalog is (800) 258-0929.

Library of Congress Catalog Number: 2004093884

ISBN: 0-87349-730-9

Designed by Donna Mummery
Edited by Tom Collins

Printed in the United States of America

Contents

About the Author and Photographer

Robert Pripps

Author Robert N. Pripps worked for 36 years in test engineering and marketing in the aviation industry. He earned his B. S. degree from Northern Illinois University, and a Certificate in Aeronautical Engineering. He retired at age 55 to begin a second career writing about historic, collectable and antique tractors. Bob has authored 25 books on tractors, most of them with photographer Andrew Morland.

Born on a small farm in Northern Wisconsin in 1932, Bob now resides almost within sight of his original place of birth.

Bob's interest in tractors began early. His dad had inherited a 1920 JT crawler from his father. The JT and a Russell grader were used in area road building and maintenance.

Later, when his dad became a State of Wisconsin Forest Ranger, Bob was exposed to even more trucks and crawler tractors. At age nine, he was allowed to disk a fire lane using an Allis-Chalmers crawler. At age 12, Bob's life was threatened when his mitten was caught on a power-take-off shaft. The incident resulted in the loss of his right thumb.

As a high school in Eagle River, Wisconsin, Bob earned a private pilot's license prior to his graduation in 1950. Just three years later, he had a commercial pilot's license with a multi-engine rating. That same year, he married Janice, a union that has produced three sons and grandchildren.

Bob has owned a variety of tractors over the years, usually no more than two at a time. His recent tractors include a Ford-Ferguson, restored to better-than-new condition, and a Massey-Ferguson MF-85 work tractor, used on his 55-acre maple forest, which he says produces 175 gallons of maple syrup each spring.

Andrew Morland

Photographer Andrew Morland was born after World War II in Southern England. He studied art and photography at Taunton College of Art in Somerset and at London College of Printing. Since graduation, he has worked as a freelance photographer, traveling throughout Europe and North America. His many works have included photographs in more than 50 tractor books and regular contributions to the magazines *Tractor and Machinery* and *Classic Tractor*. He has authored numerous books on cars, trucks, and motorcycles as well.

Andrew is himself a collector. The garage of his 17th-century thatch-roofed cottage in Somerset contains an Essex automobile, several vintage MGs and a variety of old motorcycles.

He says his ancestor, Samuel Morland, produced the first working internal combustion engine in the 1600s. However, the engine didn't run for long since its fuel was an equivalent of dynamite! Samuel Morland also was known in England and France as a builder of water pumps.

Andrew and his wife, Katherine, enjoy touring and rallying in their MGs, sailing and gardening. Their daughter Hannah is a college student.

Foreword and Acknowledgements

This is primarily a data book. The old saying "Bad data is worse than none" has been on my mind as I prepared this book. The tractor performance data listed is from University of Nebraska tests. Note, this data was not corrected for the effects of pressure and temperature and it will differ from Deere numbers. I have found that serial number versus year model information for Deere tractors is confusing. Even Deere-published numbers don't always agree. Barring typos, I think the numbers presented here are accurate as compared with the official Deere Serial Number Register. These numbers don't always agree with other published material, or with previous books I have authored, but I will stand behind them.

When in doubt about data to be presented in this book, I have taken as authoritative, the writings of Messrs. Richard Hain, J.R. Hobbs, Ralph Hughes and *Green Magazine's* Mr. Thinker. Especially, Mr. Thinker! Seriously, I find the *Green Magazine*, for which the foregoing write, has the right balance between "Correctness" (which can be overdone) and accuracy. The magazine is a must-read for any Deere aficionado. I found their information was very helpful.

Finally, when one ponders the changes in tractors in the 55 years covered by this book it is mind-boggling. Tractors went from as little as 10 hp to over 200. They grew from a two-speed power shift used on a 1917 Dain to the eight-speed Power-Shift of 1972.

During that time, the United States was involved in two world wars, a great depression, and the challenges of the cold war. The basic tractor morphed from a frame, wheels and an engine, to that which resembled a foreshortened truck with big back wheels, to the tricycle configuration, to the utility configuration, to the unbelievably big articulated four-wheel drive 7020. Through it all, Deere's management, engineering, and service people kept customers coming back for the next models. In doing so, the customers prospered and fed America and a good part of the world.

One can only be amazed at the amount of personal labor that went into the making of a loaf of bread, or similar "from-planting-to the-table" endeavors, in the days before the tractor. The advent of the reliable tractor started the farmer on the road out of a mere subsistence existence and into the status of respected businessman enjoyed today.

Of course the changes in the subsequent 30-plus years since 1972 are even greater than those of the 55 years before. That, however, is another story.

A word of thanks from the author (and photographer) to the collectors of the beautifully restored John Deere tractors shown on the following pages. The collectors went to a lot of trouble getting the tractors out for us, washing them and moving them around for the best light, and they often took us to their friend's places where we found more tractors. These are the true experts. Without the knowledge they shared with this author, this book would have been mostly pictures.

Also, thanks to writers who paved the way with their excellent books that I used as references: Randy Leffingwell, Ralph Sanders, Don MacMillan, Chester Peterson Jr., Rod Beemer, Lorry Dunning and Chuck Wendel. A special thanks to the *Green Magazine* writers mentioned before.

Robert N. Pripps
Springstead, Wisconsin
2004

Deere president William Butterworth (son-in-law of Charles Deere) considered himself responsible both for the welfare of the company and for the fortunes of the Deere family. He was not one to take a "flyer" into the tractor business in 1917.

Board members, who included Deere family members, did not share his reluctance. Stephen Velie, John Deere's son-in-law, had died in 1895. Willard Velie, Stephen's youngest son, took his father's place on the Deere board and also in the Velie family business. The Velies were manufacturing the Velie Biltwell 12-24 farm tractor that was selling reasonably well for around $1,600.

Willard Velie was adamant Deere should go after the tractor market wholeheartedly with the Dain design. He made the point that the Dain was a much more capable tractor and the price was about the same.

Butterworth had authorized the manufacture of 100 Dain tractors, but without a serious commitment to volume production, Velie was sure cost estimates wouldn't be met. It was at this point that Frank Silloway, Deere & Company's head of sales, announced to the board the Waterloo Gasoline Engine Company was for sale. It had been manufacturing a fairly successful tractor. The board instructed Silloway to check it out and report back.

Silloway found the Waterloo outfit was for sale because the owner wanted to retire. He learned the company had sold almost 7,000 of its Waterloo Boy tractors in the past two years and that the company facilities included factory space, a foundry, and an engineering department. Silloway also learned it could be bought for $2,350,000.

Deere couldn't deny it seemed like a good deal with the operation in place and already into volume production. Waterloo was about 150 miles from Moline, and Butterworth still wasn't sure. He was afraid of alienating plow business from the few tractor makers that didn't offer implements. An option-to-buy was taken.

During the interim, 100 Dain tractors were manufactured and sent to dealers. Silloway kept up his mantra through a series of memos and letters to Butterworth and various board members and dealers. On March 14, 1918, Butterworth got a telephone call from the owner of the Waterloo Gasoline Engine Company advising him Deere's option ran out that day. Butterworth hastily called a board meeting and took a vote.

The results were unanimous in favor of going ahead with the purchase. Even President Butterworth voted in the affirmative. Now Deere was in the tractor business.

The Waterloo Gasoline Engine Company was the heir of the first gasoline tractor able to go backwards as well as forward, the 1892 Froelich. When the buyers of the Froelich couldn't make them work as well as the inventor, the company retreated to the stationary engine business and Mr. Froelich went on to other things.

After a time, interest was rekindled. Since their engines were successful, why not mount one on a chassis as Froelich had done. Several iterations made it plain

Waterloo Gasoline Engine Company was the heir to the Froelich, the first gasoline tractor to go forward and backward.

Deere continued to make two versions of the Waterloo Boy, the Model R and the Model N.

that the task was not that simple. Two-cycle engines were tried. Crawlers were tried. Horizontally opposed engines were tried. Single-front-wheel designs were tried.

In 1911, the Associated Manufacturing Company of Waterloo found itself in financial trouble and sold off its foundry to the Waterloo Gasoline Engine Company to raise cash. Along with the foundry came a tractor project then underway, called the Big Chief.

Louis Witry, the main engineer for Waterloo Gasoline Engine Company, took the Big Chief on as a project. The Big Chief was equipped with a horizontally-opposed, two-cylinder, four-cycle engine.

This engine was too wide to fit between the back wheels and was mounted forward in the frame. Traction suffered and excessive gearing was required to get the power to the rear axle. Witry decided to make a two-cylinder, side-by-side engine, in the fashion of early Ford and International Harvester engines that would fit between the back wheels.

In these engines, the pistons operated in unison

allowing one, or the other cylinder to fire each revolution. This scheme required heavy counterweights, which never completely damped out the vibrations. Witry elected to have his pistons operate in "opposition" (or as some have said, boxer-style). While the cylinder firing was uneven, balance was good and size was reduced.

With the new engine, the tractor was renamed the "Waterloo Boy," thought to be a play on the words "water boy," after the company's successful line of Waterloo Boy farm engines (many of which were used to pump water) and earlier tractor experiments.

To differentiate from earlier tractor experiments, this new tractor with the Witry engine was given the designation Model R. The first example was given the Serial Number 1026. It, and others like it, was offered for sale for $750 in 1914.

Although it was off to a slow start, the Model R was selling well by 1916. A process of more-or-less continuous improvement was adopted, but significant changes were recorded in the serial number register as "style" changes A through M.

The year 1914 was also the year that World War I started in Europe. Soon food production in Britain was threatened by a shortage of men and horses, gone to war. Imports were also threatened by the German U-boat menace. The British Ministry of Munitions, by 1917, was importing all the tractors from the U.S. they could get, many of which were Waterloo Boys. L.J. Martin's Overtime Tractor Company took some of the Waterloo Boy tractors imported. Martin repainted and renamed these as "Overtime" tractors, although the Waterloo serial number was retained.

The Model R was a good tractor by the standards of the day, but by 1917, competition from some 160 companies in the business was strong. Customers were complaining that the single-speed transmission did not offer enough flexibility. Some competitors were offering three-speed gearboxes. A new version, called the Model N was introduced with two-speeds forward.

Model R and N tractors were built together until unique R parts were used up. The process of continuous improvement was continued until the Model N was replaced by the John Deere Model D in 1924. Even then, a block of serial numbers was taken out of the D sequence and used for a final run of "Boys" to use up the remaining parts inventory.

The Waterloo Boy Model N was the first tractor to be tested by the University of Nebraska. The state had just passed a law that farm tractors had to undergo and pass a rigorous test regimen before they could be sold to the public in that state.

The Waterloo Boy logo used a young farm boy and reminded buyers of a successful line of engines often used to pump water.

Overall years built: 1914-1924
Built at: Waterloo, Iowa
Number built: R 9,310
                  N 21,392

Available configurations:
1914-1915: Model R, Type A to D
    5.50 x 7.00 bore and stroke, 330 cid 700 rpm,
    integral head and block, chain steer
1915: Model R, Type E
    6.00 x 7.00 bore and stroke, 396 cid, 750 rpm,
    integral head and block, upright fuel tank
1915-1916: Model R, Type F & G
    Solid front axle
1916: Model R, Type H
    Separate head and block
1916: Model R, Type I
    2" semi-floating rear axle
1916: Model R, Type J
    Horizontal fuel tank
1916-1917: Model R, Type K & L
    Internal engine changes, 2.5" rear axle
1917-1918: Model R, Type M
    6.5 x 7.00 bore and stroke, 465cid
1917-1924: Model N
• 8378 first serial number, larger radiator, two-speed
  transmission, fuel tank raised twice in 1919.
• S/N 18720, crankshaft counterweight moved
  outside.
• S/N 19009, fan and water pump combined.
• S/N 19732, auto-type steering option.
• S/N 26174, "auto-steer" standard.
• S/N 30400 last Model N before John Deere
  Model D production. Waterloo Boy Model N
  S/N 31321-31412 made after start of Model D
  production.

Wheel Size:
    Front steel: 28 x 6 inches
    Rear steel: 52 x 12 inches

Engine: Side-by-side horizontal, four-cycle, pistons
    operating in opposition.
Number of Cylinders: 2
Bore & Stroke: 5.50x 7.00 inches (early), 6.00 x
    7.00 inches (mid), 6.5 x 7.00 inches (late)
Displacement: 330, 396 and 465 cid
Rated RPM: 700 rpm (to Style D) and 750 rpm
    (Style E through Model N)
Compression Ratio: 3.91:1
Cooling: Water pump
Fuel Tank: 20 gal.
Length: 143 inches (Model R), 132 inches (Model
    N)
Transmission:
    Single-speed: 2.5mph, reverse 2.5mph
    Two-speed: 1 2.25 mph
               2 3.00 mph
               Reverse: 2.25 mph

Weight, basic:
    Model R 6,200 lbs.
    Model N 6,180lbs.

Price, new: $ 750 in 1914
                $ 1,050 in 1923

Nebraska Test Data
Test No.: 01
Test Date: April 1920
Maximum belt hp: 25
Maximum available drawbar pull: 2,900 lbs.
specific fuel consumption (hp.-hrs./gal.) 6.83
Weight as tested (lbs.): 6,470

The R was a single-speed version with first a 333-cid two-cylinder side-by-side horizontal engine and later a similar 395-cid engine.

The Waterloo Boy Model R was offered in series A through M from 1914 through 1918. This is an M series version of the famed tractor.

I think it is safe to eliminate the horse, the mule, the bull team, and the woman, so far as generally furnishing motive power is concerned," wrote Willard L. Velie (pronounced Veely), chairman of Deere's executive committee in 1918.

His memo was to the Deere board of directors in complaint that the company's approach to tractor manufacture had been tepid, at best. His letter continued:

"I cannot refrain from remarking that we should build tractors largely and whole-heartedly, or dismiss the matter as inconsequential and immaterial."

Velie's writings point out the difficulty that Deere, Inc. had getting into the tractor business and how different the times were, especially his comment about women providing motive power. It is hard to understand today, when the words "John Deere" are virtually synonymous with "farm tractor." In 1918, the decision to get into tractors was not an easy one to make.

First, the greatest holdout was that William Butterworth, President of Deere, was responsible for the fortunes of the heirs of John and Charles Deere. Butterworth had seen the company prosper through careful and conservative management. He was reluctant to risk the financial security of the Deere family by changing that approach.

Second, in 1918, there were five or six "full-line" implement companies that also offered tractors. At the same time, there were nearly 200 companies offering tractors only, including Ford and General Motors. These tractor companies were allies of Deere in the competition with the full-line companies.

Third, while Deere's dealers were clamoring for a tractor to sell, they were adamant that it be a good one for a reasonable price. They had seen full-line dealers lose sales of disks, threshers and the like, because of a poorly performing tractor.

Fourth, America was now involved in World War I. This meant upheaval of production schedules due to war production and loss of manpower to the war effort.

The Dain shown here is one of only two complete examples left. This one is owned by the Northern Illinois Steam Power Club of Sycamore, Illinois. The other is owned by Deere, Inc. and is on display in the Deere Pavilion in Moline, Illinois.

Built in 1917 before the acquisition of the Waterloo Boy outfit, the Dain (named for a Deere director that designed and tested it) was a three-wheel machine with all three powered through chain drives.

Burton Peek, Deere's sales manager, had in fact taken a temporary job with the War Production Board in Washington, DC. Frank Silloway replaced him.

As early as 1912, the Deere board had adopted a resolution to produce a "tractor plow" at once. Subsequently, at least twelve tractors of various designs had been built and tested, at a cost of around a quarter-million dollars. The best of the lot was the tractor designed by creative board member Joseph Dain.

In 1918, the board timidly allowed the manufacture on 100 of the Dain-designed John Deere AWD tractors, even though its price would have to be double the target price of $750. This decision by the board was what prompted Velie's bluntly-worded January 1918 memo. His point was that committing to only 100 tractors guaranteed the target price would never be approached and that the tractor would be a money-loser.

Work on the Dain AWD tractor began in 1914. The next year a prototype was displayed for the Board. Dain was instructed to continue development "…until he (Dain) considers it perfected."

By the end of 1915, Dain reported he had built three tractors, two with friction drives and one with gear drive. They were exceeding performance expectations. Ten more experimental models were authorized, along with the development of a new more powerful engine commissioned from experienced engineer Walter McVicker. (The first tractors had Waukesha engines.) Dain vigorously pursued testing in various types of soils in different parts of the country.

In October 1917, Joseph Dain came down with pneumonia following a cold and wet week in the field and soon died.

Testing continued, and in November 1917, the building of 100 production tractors was authorized. Only four months later, in March 1918, Deere bought the Waterloo Gas Engine Company, maker of the Waterloo Boy tractor. The 100 Dain-AWD tractors were finished and sent to a dealer. Their disposition seems to have been lost to antiquity. The whereabouts of only three serial numbers is known.

There were two forward speeds on the Dain-John Deere AWD that propelled the tractor to 2.6 mph.

The Dain-John Deere Model AWD
Data and Specifications

Years built: 1918-1919

Built at: East Moline, Illinois

Drive system:
Three wheels, All-Wheel Drive (AWD)

Wheels:
Front: Two steel, 38 x 8 inches
Rear: Single steel, 40 x 20 inches

Engine: Deere-McVicker, four-cylinder vertical, gasoline
Bore & Stroke: 4.5 x 6.0 inches
Displacement: 381.7 cid
Rated RPM: 800
Ignition: Magneto (KW)
Cooling: Water pump

Length: 150 inches
Width: 76 inches
Height (to top of radiator): 57 inches

Transmission:
Two-speed, Power Shift

Gear	Speed (both forward and reverse)
1	2 mph
2	2.62 mph

Belt Pulley: 30 x 8 in., left side; 2190 fpm

Steering: Via front wheels through universal joints. Ratchets in each front wheel, no differential. Worm and sector gear steering.

Performance: (Not tested at the University of Nebraska)

Maximum belt horsepower: 24

Maximum drawbar horsepower: 12

Shipping weight: 4,600 lbs.

Price: $1,500

Serial Numbers: 191800-191899
S/N 191834 owned by Northern Illinois Steam Power Club, Sycamore, Illinois
S/N 191861 owned by Ken Layher, Nebraska (parts)
S/N 191879 owned by Deere & Company

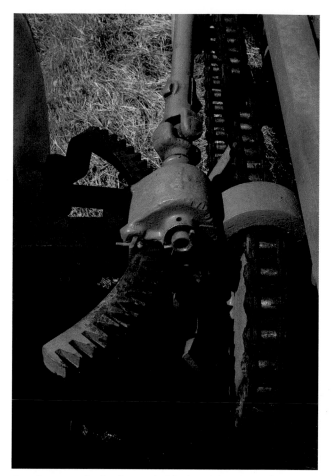

Steering was via the front wheels through universal joints. About 100 of these were built and sold before Deere recognized that the cost of producing them was too high to be profitable.

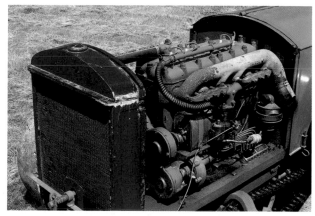

The engine was designed for Deere by Walter McVicker. A two-speed planetary transmission was used.

Overtime Model R

The Overtime Tractor was a rebadged version of the Waterloo Boy R and N models that was sold in Great Britain and Ireland. John Deere of Great Britain and Ireland credits the Overtime with helping the British and Irish win World War I by helping to produce food used in the home front and in the war effort.

The Overtime R and N tractors, like the Waterloo Boy, had push rods, rocker arms, and valve stems that were exposed. Also, it required lubrication by hand during operation.

A London importer was L.J. Martin, whose firm was called "The Overtime Tractor Company." Martin brought some 4,000 Waterloo Boy tractors in from John Deere, both R and N models, and re-named them "Overtime."

During World War I, Great Britain imported all of the tractors it could get from America. Other than the classy name stencil, they were the same as the Waterloo Boys.

The Overtime R was a single-speed version with a 395 cid two-cylinder side-by-side horizontal engine. The Model N had a two-speed transmission and a 465 cid engine of the same type.

The John Deere Model D enjoyed a 30-year production run, from 1923 to 1953. During that time it was continually improved, yet stayed unmistakably the Model D.

The D was originally conceived by the Waterloo Gasoline Engine Company as a replacement for their line of Waterloo Boy tractors. John Deere Sales Manager Frank Silloway, and others in top management at Deere, had been struggling with experimental tractor designs for 10 years.

When rumors were intercepted that the Waterloo Boy outfit was for sale Deere jumped on it. For $2.1 million Deere acquired all the assets of the Waterloo Gasoline Engine Company, including the experimental tractor that would become the Model D. Deere and Company tractor production has continued in Waterloo, Iowa, to this day.

When Deere took over the Waterloo company in 1918, it continued production of the Waterloo Boy tractors and also the development of the new model destined to replace the "Boy."

Waterloo identified their tractor styles (models) by letter. Experimental styles A through C were built and tested. Style D was considered ready for production in 1923, and became the John Deere Model D. It was Serial Number 401 of these experimental tractors.

Waterloo Boy tractors were up to Serial Number 28000+ by then, so Deere arbitrarily assigned the prefix number "30" to 401 for the first Model D S/N of 30401. The idea was to leave what was thought to be a sufficient gap to allow the company to finish out the Waterloo Boy production.

Later, when Waterloo Boy production reached S/N 30400, Deere jumped to a block of numbers for

Production of the Model D tractor began in 1923, overlapping the Waterloo Boy Model N, which it was intended to replace. The Waterloo Gasoline Engine Company started the design and testing of this replacement before they were acquired by Deere.

A revised air cleaner and longer fenders than the '23 model, and a larger spoked flywheel than the '25 model were features of the John Deere Model D tractor.

the Waterloo Boy from 31320 to 31412. That means 92 numbers are missing from the D sequence.

International Harvester, Ford, and Allis Chalmers dominated competition in the tractor business in the early 1920s. Henry Ford, with his inexpensive Fordson had taken over the lead in production numbers. The other makers were forced to adopt Ford's features and production methods to stay in the game.

Deere incorporated the best of these, plus the best of the Waterloo Boy, into the production Model D. The Fordson contributed the frameless, or unit-frame concept. The engine and drive train castings became the tractor's frame.

As a concession to the Fordson's automobile heritage, the radiator was placed in front and a hood covered the engine. The Waterloo Boy heritage was seen in the roller-chain final drive and the reliable and gutsy two-cylinder engine.

The Waterloo Boy had also used a two-speed transmission. This was continued, though the Fordson, at nearly one-third the price, had three speeds. The end result was a well-balanced, reliable tractor that was easy

to start and could pull 75 percent of its own weight.

Deere and Company has always been noted for reinvesting in research to make its products better. By 1928 a decision was made to give the D more power by increasing the engine bore diameter by a quarter inch—from 6.5 to 6.75 inches.

This increase, along with a new Schebler carburetor, would boost the belt horsepower from 30 to 37. Other changes were made to maintain equivalent strength with the increased power, including new 20-spoke rear wheels. Late in 1928, at S/N 68880, a steel platform replaced the wood, and flat-spoke front wheels and new stronger fenders were incorporated.

The years following the Market Crash of 1929 saw tractor sales plummet to nearly zero. Deere had problems with its Model GP and was spending development money on the new Models A and B.

The Soviet Union found just what it needed in the John Deere Model D tractor and bought more than 4,000 of them for their collective farms. These sales helped considerably to provide needed cash flow for continued development of the Model D.

Another big improvement in the D appeared in the 1931 model. The biggest change was the increase in engine speed from 800 to 900 rpm. This change required a complete engine redesign with things both strengthened and enlarged.

A new Marvel-Schebler DLTX-6 carburetor completed the job of bringing the engine to over 40 hp. At the same time, the steering was revised and the front axle was strengthened. The steering wheel was moved from the left side to the right side (closer to the center, as some would say). An oil filter and an oil pressure indicator were added. Zerk lubrication fittings (that replaced the turndown grease cups) were incorporated.

By 1933, rubber tires became an option on the D. In 1934, fuel tank capacity was increased from 23.5 to 25 gallons. This required relocating the starting gas tank (now 1.5 gallons) to the outside rear of the main tank. A revised hood was also part of this change. Again in 1934, a new adjustable seat design became available at S/N 116488.

The next big change for the D came in 1935. Finally, a three-speed transmission was incorporated. This greatly improved the competitive position of the D versus the other tractors in its field. By now, some of them had gone to four speed transmissions. Other changes for 1935 included an oil-bath air cleaner, a proper oil pressure gauge, an improved muffler and a 12-spline rear axle.

Cosmetically, the "leaping deer" was now removed from its former place between the words "John" and "Deere" on the hood sides. A new three-spoke rubber-rimmed steering wheel was adopted (as old stock was used up). For 1936, a water temperature gauge was added at S/N 125430.

In 1937, transmission ratios were slightly changed and a foot-operated service brake was incorporated. Also, a new Edison-Splitdorf magneto eliminated the need for a spark control. Beginning at S/N 133201, radiator shutters replaced the curtain.

For 1939, at S/N 143800, the D received the Dreyfuss styling treatment, the fifth John Deere tractor

The engine of the Model D was of the same horizontal two-cylinder type as the Waterloo Boy, but it was larger in displacement and horsepower.

to be styled (after the Models A, B, H and L). Although not as extensive as the others, the changes did include attractive new sheet metal, a new purposeful radiator grille, and some technical improvements.

The technical improvements included relocation of the operator's seat to be directly behind the steering wheel, a new instrument panel, a revised drawbar pivoted ahead of the rear axle, a new higher platform, and fender enclosures that kept mud and debris out of the "cockpit."

An important option for the Styled D was an electrical system with a starter. The lighting option could be exercised with, or without the starter, and included headlights mounted on each fender.

A rear light was below the seat. One six-volt battery was installed for tractors with lighting only. Tractors with starters and the lighting came with a second battery.

In 1939, steel wheels were standard for the styled D, but all combinations of steel and rubber were available. For 1941, rubber became standard for a short time. Then WWII shortages prompted a return to standard steel.

Dual rear tires were also an option until the change was made to 30-inch rear wheels in 1941. New rice fenders became available at S/N 150617 to provide more clearance with the 30-inch rear tires. In 1947, rubber tires again became standard equipment with steel optional.

Production of the D continued at record levels from 1947 to 1949 with few, if any changes. With the introduction of the new Model R diesel in 1949, sales of the D fell off sharply.

Deere continued supplying Model Ds to satisfy the diminishing demand. In 1951, a factory "gasoline" option put the D in the over-50-hp class.

By the end of 1952, a last-call was issued to sales branches and production ended with S/N 191578 — or so it seemed. Then, more orders came in and the inventory of available parts in stock revealed 92 more Model Ds could be built.

The production line had already been broken down and new production had been set up where the Ds were assembled so parts were delivered to a street between two factory buildings. Workers then built Serial Numbers 191579 to 191670 outside in the street.

These "Streeter" models are among the rarest and most collectable Ds, especially since only 36 were shipped to U.S. locations. The remaining 56 were exported, with one going to Canada and the rest sent to unknown destinations.

Thus ended one of the most important chapters in history of the American farm tractor.

Characteristics of the 1924 version of the D were left-hand steering, three holes in the spokes of the steering wheel, and both the '23 and '24 models had one-piece steering shafts.

Model D
Data and Specifications

Overall Years Built: 1923-1953

Built at: Waterloo, Iowa

Available configurations:

Standard Tread, three-four plow

1923-1924: 30401-30450

6.5 x 7 engine, 800 rpm, welded front axle, left hand steering, ladder side radiator, 26-inch spoke flywheel

1924: 30451-31279

cast front axle

1924-1926: 1280-36248

24-inch spoke flywheel

1926-1927: 36249-53387

solid flywheel, keyed to shaft

1927-1930: 53388-109943

6.75 x 7 engine, solid flywheel, splined to shaft

(1931-1934): 109944-119099

900 rpm, right-hand steer, intake and exhaust stacks above hood

1935-1938: 119945-143799

three-speed transmission

1939-1953: 143800-191578

Styled

1953: 191579-191670

"Streeters"

Wheel/ Tire Size:

Front Steel: 28 x 5

Rear Steel: 46 x 12

Front Rubber (low pressure): 7.50-18

Front Rubber (high pressure): 36 x 5

Rear Rubber (low pressure): 13.5-28/12.75-28/13-30*

Rear Rubber (high pressure): 42 x 9

The change was made from 28 to 30-inch rear wheels at S/N 150617 for tractors without individual (steering) brakes. Tractors with individual brakes received 30-inch wheels at S/N 151957. The dual rear wheel option was not available with 30-inch rears.

Engine: Side-by-side horizontal diesel, overhead valve, four-cycle

Number of Cylinders: 2

Bore & Stroke: 6.50 x 7 inches (early), 6.75 x 7.00 inches (late)

Displacement: 465/501 cid

Rated RPM: 800 rpm (early), 900 rpm (late)

Compression Ratio: 3.91:1

Cooling: Thermosyphon

Fuel Tank: 18 gal. (early), 25 gal. (late)

Height (to top of radiator): 56 in. to 1930, then 58 in. to 1934 and 61in. to 1953

Length: 109 in. to 1930, then 130 in. to 1953

Transmission:

Two-Speed:

1	2.5 mph
2	3.25 mph
reverse	2.0 mph

Three-Speed *	1935	1937
1	2.5 mph	3.0
2	3.5 mph	4.0
3	5.0 mph	5.25
reverse	1.5 mph	1.5

*Drive sprocket options could increase speeds by as much as 32 percent.

Weight, basic:

1924: 4,090 lbs.

1927: 4,150 lbs.

1935: 5,520 lbs.

1939: 5,880 lbs.

Price, new: $1,000, 1923

$2,124, 1953

(Standard equipment on steel)

Nebraska Test Data

Test No. 102
Date: 4-1924
Max. belt hp.: 30.4
Max. available drawbar pull: 3,227
Specific fuel consumption hp.-hrs.gal.: 9.03
Weight as tested (lbs.): 4,260

Test No. 146
Date: 10-1927
Max. belt hp.: 36.98
Max. available drawbar pull: 4,462
Specific fuel consumption hp.-hrs.gal.: 10.74
Weight as tested (lbs.): 4,917

Test No. 236
Date: 7-1935
Max. belt hp.: 40.11
Max. available drawbar pull: 4,037
Specific fuel consumption hp.-hrs.gal.: 10.14
Weight as tested (lbs.): 5,690

Test No. 350
Date: 7-1940
Max. belt hp.: 40.24
Max. available drawbar pull: 4,830
Specific fuel consumption hp.-hrs.gal.: 10.14
Weight as tested (lbs.): 8,125

Model D Serial Number vs. Year Model

Year	Beginning Serial Number
1924	30401*
1925	31280
1926	35309
1927	43410
1928	53388
1929	71645
1930	95367
1931	109944
1932	115509
1933	115665
1934	116273
1935	119100
1936	125079
1937	130700
1938	138413
1939	142300-143799 Unstyled
1939	143800 Styled
1940	146500
1941	148872
1942	151887
1943	154470
1944	155029
1945	158454
1946	161701
1947	164897
1948	171956
1949	180812
1950	187703
1951	189600
1952	190961
1953	191405-191670

Tractors built in 1923 are considered 1924 models.

John Deere's design was unique in that it was designed for three-row cultivation, rather than two.
Owner: Layher Collection

By the mid-1920s, Deere was well established among the ranks of tractor makers. Their Model D, which was considered a lightweight tractor, was setting the standard for pulling power, economy and reliability.

Surprisingly, auto magnate Henry Ford's even-lighter Fordson tractor was first in sales, not only in the U.S, but also world wide. International Harvester was in second place, Deere third, and Case fourth.

The trend to lighter, less expensive tractors started in 1913 with the Little Bull tractor. It was a one-wheel drive outfit that sold for $395. The Bull knocked Harvester out of first place for a time, but poor performance and reliability soon spelled its demise.

Another 1913 tractor innovation was the Moline Universal, the world's first "all purpose" tractor. By 1925, it too had gone the way of the Dodo bird, a casualty of its high $1,300 price.

Interestingly, International Harvester purchased Moline's manufacturing plants—in Moline and Rock Island, Illinois. Deere's home territory! These factories were to be the manufacturing place for I-H's new "all-purpose" Farmall tractor.

While several tractor manufacturers, including Deere, had only one model on the market, Deere's archrival, I-H, was fielding three. Deere's management decided to investigate the market for a smaller, lighter, cheaper tractor with the all-purpose characteristics of the Farmall (which had entered volume production in 1926).

They decided the ideal all-purpose tractor would be able to do all the plowing and pulling chores plus the flat-belt work done by traditional tractors. In addition, it would be able to do cultivating and planting, and would be equipped with a rear PTO for powering grain harvesters, pickers and mowers. It would have steering brakes for row-end maneuverability.

Like several other manufacturers, Deere had embarked on motor cultivator projects. While these didn't pan out for anybody, they helped form the basis for on-going, all-purpose tractor designs. The Farmall had its heritage in such a motor cultivator.

Deere engineers also began where motor cultivator efforts left off. Experimental "all crop" tractors were built in 1926. Improved versions followed in 1927 and were followed by 75 more later the same year. The experimental tractors were now called the Model C.

Model Cs were replaced in 1928 by a tractor called the GP (General Purpose), renamed because "D" and "C" sounded so nearly the same.

The Model C was introduced in 1927 and was produced through 1935. The C/GP was Deere's answer to the International Harvester's new Farmall "general-purpose" tractor.
Owner: Layher Collection

Famed Deere tractor engineer, Theo Brown, elected to go with a wide front end on the new tractor for two reasons. With an arched front axle able to straddle a row, three rows could be cultivated (or planted). The Farmall's narrow front ran between two rows and each was cultivated (or planted) as it went. The Deere GP offered a 50% increase in productivity over the Farmall.

The fixed rear tread width and narrow front of the Farmall led to side-draft problems when plowing with a two-bottom plow. The GP's right front wheel ran in the previous furrow providing virtually automatic guidance and eliminating side-draft problems.

Theo Brown scored another first on the Model C/GP. He invented the powered implement lift. This device clutched in engine power to raise the cultivator at the end of the row. The turn at the row's end could be made without stopping. The feet tripped the lift and actuated the turning brake, while the hands steered and operated the throttle and hand clutch as needed.

There were some changes between the Model C and the new Model GP of 1928. The C had used a single spring-loaded strut to hold the pan-type seat — called the "pogo stick support." This was replaced by a more conventional leaf-spring design. The wooden steering wheel was replaced by an all-metal design, which better withstood outside storage. There were minor changes to the front axle and exhaust manifold.

In service, early GPs were somewhat disappointing. Despite many years of testing and design iterations prior to volume production, field failures continued at a high rate.

Deere assigned field men to repair tractors free of charge, but the downtime was hurting Deere's reputation. And, while the tractor sent to the University of Nebraska for testing made almost 25 belt hp, most of the production models could only manage to produce 20 or 22 hp. Drawbar pull was only marginally better than the poorly-balanced lightweight Fordson.

The Model C/GP was unique in that it was the only horizontal Deere two-cylinder engine to use the L-head design. It was also the only Deere tractor to use a mechanical implement lift.
Owner: Layher Collection

The one shown is Serial Number 200201. The official designation was changed from C to GP in August 1928.
Owner: Layher Collection

These early Model GPs had a 312-cid side-valve (L-Head) engine like the Model C.

By 1929, it was recognized that the air cleaner location was the cause of some of the problems. Located between the cylinder head and radiator, the intake picked up an inordinate amount of dirt and debris. This led to reduced performance and shortened engine life. After Serial Number 212555, a tall, vertical intake pipe was incorporated which was located on the pulley side. The exhaust now came out of a pipe on the flywheel side.

In July 1930, the first of the 6 x 6 engines (the bore diameter was increased .25 in. to 6.00 inches) appeared on the new GPWT, or Wide-Tread. This was a version of the GP in the tricycle configuration.

The new engine had a reduced compression ratio, eliminating the need for the water injection system, which had been troublesome. The dramatic increase in bore diameter more than made up for the power loss due to the reduced compression ratio.

The GPWT was a concession made to farmers who did not take readily to the three-row concept. The GPWTs had a 76-inch rear tread and used a different serial numbering sequence.

For the 1931 model year, all GPs got the 6 x 6 engine, which included the new "crossover" manifolds. Other improvements were also incorporated at that time in the steering, final drives, cooling system, and engine.

It should be noted the country was in the grips of the Great Depression. Since 1930, Deere was finding itself with an inventory of unsold tractors. Some of the GPWTs in stock were converted to a narrower 68-inch rear tread for use in the potato fields of the Northeast. These were given a special serial number sequence and are called GP-P, for potato.

The Model GP tractor went through several iterations between 1928 and 1935. At first, no air stacks were provided. In late 1929, a tall air intake was added.

Overall years built: 1927 – 1935
Built at: Waterloo, Iowa
Model variations:
All crop/ Model C
    S/N 101-125 (experimental), 1927
Pre-production Model C
    S/N 200001-200010 (76 tractors), 1927
Production Model C
    S/N 200111-200202, 1927-1928
Model GP
    S/N 200211-223793 (5.75 in. bore), 1928-1930*
Model GPWT
    S/N 400000-402039 (5.75 in. bore), 1929-1930 (76 in. rear tread)
Model GP-P
    S/N 5000-5202, 1930 (68 in. rear tread)
Model GPO
    S/N 15000-15732, 1931-1935
Model GPWT
    S/N 402040-404809 (6.00 in. bore), 1930-1932
Model GPWT
    S/N 404810-405252 (overhead steering), 1932-1933
Model GP
    S/N 224100-230745 (6.00 in. bore), 1931-1935

*About 23 GP tricycle tractors were built in 1928 and 1929.

Wheels/Tires:
Model: C/GP
    Front steel: 24 x 6 inch
    Front rubber: 6.00 x 16
    Rear steel: 42.75 x 10 inch
    Rear rubber: 10.00 x 32

Model: GPO
    Front steel: 24 x 6 inch
    Rear steel: 42.75 x 10 inch

Model: GPWT
    Front steel: 24 x 6 inch
    Rear steel: 44 x 10 inch

Engine:
   Type: Two-cylinder, four-stroke, horizontal side-by-side with pistons operating in opposition.
   Side valves (L-head).
   Bore and stroke:*
      1927-1930:   5.75 x 6.00 in.
      1931-1935:   6.00 x 6.00 in.
   Displacement:
      1927-1930:   311.6 cid
      1931-1935:   339.3 cid
   Rated RPM:
      1927-1930:   900 rpm
      1931-1935:   950 rpm
   Basic weight:
      1927-1930:   4,260 lbs.
      1931-1935:   4,740 lbs.
   Height (to top of hood)
      1927-1930:   55.5 in.
      1931-1935:   55.5 in. (standard tread)
   Length
      1927-1930:   112
      1931-1935:   112 (standard tread)
   Price (new)
      1927-1930: $ 800
      1931-1935: $ 1,200

Transmission:

	Gear	Speed (mph)
1927-1930:		
	1	2.50
	2	3.12
	3	4.33
	Reverse	2.00
1931-1935:		
	1	2.25
	2	3.00
	3	4.00
	Reverse	1.75

Year Model vs. Beginning Serial Number

Year	Serial Number	
1928	200211	Standard
1929	201336	Standard
	400000	Wide-Tread
1930	212038	Standard
	400936	Wide-Tread
1931	223803	Standard
	402741	Wide-Tread
	15000	Orchard
1932	228666	Standard
	404770	Wide-Tread
	15226	Orchard
1933	229051	Standard
	405110	Wide-Tread
	15387	Orchard
1934	229216	Standard
	15412	Orchard
1935	230514	Standard
	15589	Orchard

Nebraska Test Data

Test No. 153
Date: 10-1928
Max. belt hp.: 24.97
Max. drawbar pull (lbs.): 2,489
Specific fuel consumption hp.-hrs./gal.: 9.18
Weight as tested (lbs.): 4,500

Test No. 190
Date: 5-1931
Max. belt hp.: 25.36
Max. drawbar pull (lbs.): 2,853
Specific fuel consumption hp.-hrs./gal.: 9.50
Weight as tested (lbs.): 4,925

Shown is a John Deere Model GP built in 1929. It has a nice paint job, round-spoke wheels and rubber tires. The decals are incorrect.

The steep slopes of the western orchards made the crawler configuration desirable. After pioneering the crawler using the GPO tractor, Lindeman switched to the John Deere Model BO for most of its conversions.

Deere's Model GP had proven disappointing in sales and in the field. By the late 1920s, the new Farmall was eating its lunch. Despite deepening shadows of the Great Depression as the decade turned to the 1930s, Deere decided to take a clean-sheet look at a new all-purpose tractor. Some of the features they sought include:

• Valve in head engine design.
• Faster engine, less displacement.
• Better power-to-weight ratio.
• Straight axle with splined rear wheel adjustments.
• All-gear final drive.
• Over-engine steering and tricycle configuration.
• Four-speed transmission.

Work began in 1931 with an experimental tractor, designated FX, completed by December. It was a 30 hp tractor.

Because of the Great Depression, Deere considered two factors. The market was larger for a tractor with a 24 hp engine. Also, it was decided to stay with the two-cylinder engine, rather than undertake expensive and costly engine development.

Several other "X" models were built and tested and by 1933, it was decided to build 10 prototypes, designated "AA" models.

Some of these had three-speed transmissions while others had a new four-speed unit. Test results were generally satisfactory but some nagging problems

A watershed year for John Deere was 1934 with the introduction of its classic Model A. The A was offered in every conceivable configuration from Hi-Crop to Standard-tread. Shown is the 1935 AW or A, Wide-front.

This is considered to be a "late-styled" Model A. It was built in 1949.

persisted including excessive oil consumption and low horsepower on some engines. Eventually, engineers solved all the problems except for an occasionally low-powered engine. At that point, it was decided to increase the bore diameter by .25 inches and live with the fluctuations.

By March 1934, it was decided to release four pre-production versions for testing. Serial Numbers 410008-410011 were built and tested in actual farming conditions.

In late March 1934, Serial Number 410012, the first production John Deere Model A General Purpose was shipped to a customer.

A major feature of the A-GP was the optional hydraulic implement lift. There had been mechanical lifts before, but this was the first to use smooth hydraulic power. A big feature was its capability to softly lower the implement, rather than simply dropping it from its full height.

Other changes were made mid-year as problems arose. Bosses were added to the rear axle for fenders at S/N 410130. At S/N 413879 the fuel filler cap was offset to the left to get it out from under the steering shaft. AW and AN (A, Wide front/narrow-single front wheel) versions were added in mid-1935.

Front wheels (for rubber) were changed from spoke-type to pressed steel at S/N 445325 and the radiator curtain was replaced by shutters at S/N 450832.

Model year 1938 saw the introduction of the AWH

and ANH versions with higher crop clearance. The last unstyled Model A was S/N 476221, built in June 1938.

Next came the beautiful versions of the Model A designed by Henry Dreyfuss. Known as the "Early-Styled" tractors, these were a little different under the skin. The styled model B required so much engineering attention that the A got virtually none. The first styled A was rolled out on Aug. 1, 1938. Due to continuing hard times for farmers, some 472 unsold, unstyled Model As were recalled and rebuilt as styled tractors.

For 1940, the engine displacement was increased from 309 to 321 cid. This was accomplished by increasing the stroke from 6.5 to 6.75 inches. The A now was a three-plow tractor in most conditions, making it more favorably positioned versus the new Farmall M. With the increased horsepower, the PTO shaft diameter was increased from 1.125 to 1.375 in. This size would become the industry standard.

Also new for the 1940 model year was an electric starting option. Placement of the battery behind the fuel tank required a hood extension. This extension, and tractors equipped with it, came to be known as "slant dashes."

More changes came with the 1941 version of the John Deere A. Those delivered on rubber tires now had a six-speed gearbox. This was one more than the Farmall competition, and greatly improved work output and flexibility. Between 1941 and 1947, changes were few.

At S/N 500012, five-inch head and work lights replaced the old seven-inch variety. A pressurized steel radiator was used on tractors between S/N 523600 and S/N 542699.

Starting as early as 1945, plans were made to develop an improved version of the A. Competition was making serious inroads into Deere's three-plow territory. Farmers wanted more power, comfort and convenience and they liked the convenience and flexibility of gasoline.

At least six experimental tractors were built to test new features. The design firm of Henry Dreyfuss and Associates was involved and recommended a rigidly mounted, cushioned bench seat with a backrest.

The space below the seat became the ideal location for the two six-volt batteries for the 12-volt starter. The Dreyfuss team also came up with a new pressed steel front-end support, or frame. Besides looking better, the new frame had more attachment points for implements and provided a covering for the spark plugs.

Also developed on the experimental tractors was the John Deere exclusive feature called the Roll-O-Matic system for dual tricycle front wheels. The Roll-O-Matic featured trailing links from the front spindle. These links were geared together in such a way that when one wheel was forced up by a bump, it forced the other down by means of the gears.

The result was the nose of the tractor only went up half as far as the wheel that hit the bump. The action was essentially the same as that of a wide front with a center pivot. Finally, the new cyclone combustion chamber was incorporated, boosting the gasoline-powered A

to about 40 hp. All-fuel versions, as tractors set up for distillate, were called, also got the new head design and also received a power increase.

The new A, which came to be called the "Late-Styled A," reached dealers in late March 1947. Farmers liked it and bought it to the extent that the assembly plant was running at just about maximum capacity. Specialty options were trimmed, simplifying production.

ANH and AWH versions were eliminated. Farmers could still order AN and AW models with larger tires (42 inch, instead of 38 inch). Also dropped from the option list were the special high and low speed transmissions.

A hydraulic implement lift was standard, with the new Powr-Trol optional (offering control of remote power cylinders).

Some field complaints prompted an improved A beginning with Serial Number 648000 introduced in late 1949. This version had a single shift lever and a creeper first gear, both like the Model B. Another change was a two-piece pedestal, which allowed the owner to change front-end configurations.

Other changes and improvements were introduced as time went on. At S/N 650764, a new square rear axle housing was introduced along with clamshell fenders. Distributor ignition became an option at S/N 659290. At S/N 666729, an eighteen-gallon fuel tank was added, along with a kit to change older tractors to the new larger tank. At S/N 665000, a new AH was offered with 33 inches of crop clearance.

On May 12, 1952, the last Model A left the assembly line. It was S/N 703384, a gasoline tricycle version. And so ended a 28-year production run.

The Model AW used a 321-cid two-cylinder engine with a Marvel-Schebler carburetor and a six-speed transmission.

Only 26 of these tractors were made, this one in 1938. It had the 309-cid two-cylinder engine and four-speed transmission.
Owner: Keller Collection

The John Deere Model AO is powered by a 321-cid two-cylinder engine.
Owner: Betty Norton

Model A

Data and Specifications

Overall years built: 1934 – 1952
Overall serial numbers: 410008 – 701754
Built at: Waterloo, Iowa

Front and rear axle options:

Dual Tricycle Front/ adjustable splined rear axle (A)

Standard Tread (AR), or in Orchard configuration (AO/AOS)

Adjustable Wide Front/ adjustable splined rear axle (AW)

Single Front Wheel / Adjustable splined rear axle (AN)

Adjustable Wide Front, longer spindles/ longer adjustable splined rear axle (AWH)

Single Front Wheel / adjustable splined rear axle (ANH)

Wheels/Tires:
1934-1939
Model: A
    Front steel: 24 x 4 inch
    Front rubber: 5.50 - 16
    Rear steel: 50 x 6 inch
    Rear rubber: 9/10/11.25 - 36

Model: AW
    Front steel: 24 x 4 inch
    Front rubber: 5.50 - 16
    Rear steel: 50 x 6 inch
    Rear rubber: 9/10/11.25 - 36

Model: AN
    Front steel: 24 x 8 inch
    Front rubber: 9.00 - 10
    Rear steel: 50 x 6 inch
    Rear rubber: 9/10/11.25 - 36

Model: ANH
    Front steel: N/A
    Front rubber: 7:50 - 16
    Rear steel: N/A
    Rear rubber: 9.00 - 40

Wheels/Tires (cont.):
1934-1959
Model: AWH
    Front steel: N/A
    Front rubber: 5.50 x 16
    Rear steel: N/A
    Rear rubber: 9.00 - 40

1940-1947
Model: A
    Front rubber: 5.50 - 16
    Rear rubber: 9/10/11.00 - 38

Model: AW
    Front rubber: 5.50 - 16
    Rear rubber: 9/10/11.00 - 38

Model: AN
    Front rubber: 9.00 - 10
    Rear rubber: 9/10/11.00 - 38

Model: ANH
    Front rubber: 7.50 - 16
    Rear rubber: 9:00 - 40/11.00 - 38

Model: AWH
    Front rubber: 5.50 - 16
    Rear rubber: 9:00 - 40/11.00 - 38

1947-1952
Model: A
    Front rubber: 5.50 - 16
    Rear rubber: 11.00 - 38

Model: AW
    Front rubber: 5.50 - 16
    Rear rubber: 11/12 - 38 or 12.4 - 42

Model: AN
    Front rubber: 9.00 - 10 or 7.50 - 16
    Rear rubber: 11/12 - 38 or 12.4 - 42

Model: AH
    Front rubber: 7.50 - 20
    Rear rubber: 11/12.00 - 38

Model A (Row Crop)

S/N 410000-459999 (1934-mid 1937)
    10-spline rear axles
S/N 460000-477999 (mid 1937-1939)
    12-spline rear axles
S/N 488000-703384 (1940-1952)
    15-spline rear axles

Model AR, AO, AOS

Front: Steel, spoke – 28 x 6 in. Rubber – 6.00-16
Rear: Steel, spoke – 42.75 x 10 in. Rubber
    – 11.25-24
Tread: 51 inches (AOS = 45.375 inches)

Engine Options:

Type: Two-cylinder, four-stroke horizontal, side-by-
side with pistons operating in opposition.

1934-1939

Bore & Stroke:	5.5 x 6.5 in.
Displacement:	309 cid
Rated RPM:	975 rpm

1940-1952

Bore & Stroke:	5.5 x 6.75 in.
Displacement:	321cid
Rated RPM:	975 rpm

Transmission:

Gear	Speed (mph)
1934-1940:	
1	2.33
2	3.00
3	4.75
4	6.25
Reverse	3.50
1941-1952:	
1	2.50
2	3.25
3	4.25
4	5.50
5	7.33
6	12.33
Reverse	4.00

1934-1940:	Model A	Model AO/AR
Shipping weight:	3,525 lbs.	
Length:	124 in.	124 in.
Height to radiator:	60 in.	55 in.
Price, new:	$1,050	

1941-1952:		
Shipping weight:	4,000 lbs.	3,400 lbs.
Length:	134 in.	124 in.
Height to radiator:	63 in.	55 in.
Price, new:	$2,400 (1952)	$2,300 (1951)

This Classic unstyled John Deere tractor was the ultimate row-crop tractor in 1934. The one shown has French and Hecht round-spoke wheels. It carries the AW designation because of its wide front end.

Year Model vs Beginning Serial Number

Year	Serial Number	
1934	410008	A-GP
1935	412869	A-GP
1936	424025	A-GP
	250000	AO/AR
1937	442151	A-GP
	253521	AO/AR
	AO-1000	AOS
1938	466787	A-GP
	255416	AO/AR
	AO-1539	AOS
1939	477000	A-GP
	257004	AO/AR
	AO-1725	AOS
	Note: 487250-487999 not used	
1940	488000	A-GP
	258045	AO/AR
	AO-1801	AOS
	Note: 498536-498999 not used	
1941	499000	A-GP
	260000	AO/AR
1942	510239	A-GP
	261558	AO/AR
1943	520004	A-GP
	262243	AO/AR
1944	524423	A-GP
	263223	AO/AR
	Note: 542627-542699 not used	
1945	542700	A-GP
	264738	AO/AR
1946	555334	A-GP
	265870	AO/AR
1947	569610	A-GP
	267082	AO/AR
	Note: 583327-583999 not used	
1947	584000	A-GP
	Note: The first of the "Late-Styled"	
1948	587349	A-GP
	268877	AO/AR
1949	611921	A-GP
	270646	AO/AR
1950	648000	A-GP
	272985	AO/AR
	Note: 647070-647999 not used*	
1951	666307	A-GP
	276078	AO/AR
1952	682602	A-GP
	279770	AO/AR
	Note: 700141-700199 not used,	
	703384 was last A	
1953	282551	A-GP

*Official records state the first 1950 Model A was S/N 640246, despite the rounding up of numbers to 648000 and that a number of changes were incorporated at that time. Most authorities use 648000 as the start of the 1950 model year.

Nebraska Test Data

Test Number 222 A
Date: 4-1934
Max. belt. hp.: 24.71
Max. drawbar pull (lbs.): 2,923
Specific fuel consumption hp.-hrs./gal.: 10.5 (dist.)
Weight as tested (lbs.): 4,059 (steel)

Test Number 335 A
Date: 11-1939
Max. belt. hp.: 28.93
Max. drawbar pull (lbs.): 4,110
Specific fuel consumption hp.-hrs./gal.: 11.3 (dist.)
Weight as tested (lbs.): 6,410 (rubber)

Test Number 378 AR
Date: 11-1941
Max. belt. hp.: 28.71
Max. drawbar pull (lbs.): 4,248
Specific fuel consumption hp.-hrs./gal.: 11.12 (dist.)
Weight as tested (lbs.): 4,815 (rubber)

Test Number 384 A
Date: 6-1947
Max. belt. hp.: 35.81
Max. drawbar pull (lbs.): 4,034
Specific fuel consumption hp.-hrs./gal.: 11.44 (gas.)
Weight as tested (lbs.): 5,228 (rubber)

Test Number 429 AR
Date: 10-1949
Max. belt. hp.: 36.13
Max. drawbar pull (lbs.): 4,372
Specific fuel consumption hp.-hrs./gal.: 11.74 (gas)
Weight as tested (lbs.): 7,367 (rubber)

Model A variations:

AA: 1933, 410000-410007, Prototypes
A: 1934, 410008-410011, Pre-production
A: 1934-'35, 410008-414808; Open fan shaft, 309 cid. Engine
A: 1935, 414809-, Enclosed fan shaft
A: 1938, 477000-, Early styled, 4-speed
A: 1941, 499000-, 6-speed, 321 cid. engine
A: 1947, 584000-, Late styled, pressed-steel frame
AR/AO: 1935-1936, 250000-252723, 309 cid engine, offset radiator cap
AR/AO: 1941-1949, 260000-271999, 321 cid engine
AR/AO: 1949-1953, 272000-284074, Styled

This Hi-Crop 1952 Model A was one of the last of the type, although some AO (Orchard) and AR (Standard-tread) were built in 1953.

The Hi-Crop 1952 Model A has been restored to pristine condition by Larry Maasdam of Clarion, Iowa.

Model B

The Model B has the distinction of being the best-selling John Deere tractor. In its 17-year production history it was offered in many variations, including a crawler (modified by the Lindeman Bros. of Yakima, Washington). More than 300,000 left the Waterloo Iowa factory.

The Model B was born in 1935 amidst the severe economic times of the Great Depression. It was also confronted at its birth with severe competition from the McCormick F-12 and W-12. Its predecessor in the Deere lineup (the Model GP) hadn't lived up to expectations. The Deere management Power Farming Committee decided on two brand new designs, the Models A and B.

The A (covered elsewhere) was first out of the blocks to be followed the next year by the B. Both were remarkably advanced concepts at the time and both carried the fight to the competition.

The first Model B prototypes were designated "HX." In the latter part of 1933, seven were completed for testing. The results were good enough that seven more slightly improved versions were completed by January 1934. By October 1934, the start of the 1935 model year, production versions were coming off the assembly lines.

Like the Models A and D then in production, the Model B was designed specifically to run on low-cost kerosene. It was rated for one 16-inch plow. Deere advertised the Model B had the work output of six good horses, since it didn't have to be rested. The basic general-purpose (GP), or row crop version, used a dual tricycle front end with over-engine steering.

Deere, Inc. has always been noted for building low-production variations of its tractors (to the delight of ardent collectors). The Model B was a prime example.

The first variation was the BN with a single front

The Model B came out in 1935, a year after the Model A. The B was essentially a scaled down version of the A. Production continued into 1952 with some 320,000 built. This is the very first, Serial Number 1000.
Owner: Keller Collection

This rare 1935 John Deere Model B, is a standard-tread (non-row-crop) tractor. It used the 149-cid two-cylinder engine and only 14.25 belt hp. In 1938, engine displacement was boosted to 175 cid, making 17.5 belt hp available. Owner: John Davis, Maplewood, Ohio.

wheel. It was especially made for the California vegetable growers and became known as the B Garden Tractor.

The next variation was the BW, with its adjustable wide front end. It allowed the front and rear wheels to run in the same tracks. The first 25 of these had the tread adjustment of the front axle secured with set screws. This was changed to bolts passing through the axle tubes at S/N 8974.

An odd variation of the BW was next: the BW-40, or "special narrow" BW. Special axles were used front and back, to allow tread widths as narrow as 40 inches. Maximum tread width of the BW-40 was 72 inches, but that required front extensions.

In 1934, International Harvester introduced their standard-tread version of the F-12, called the W-12. This prompted Deere engineers to look into a standard-tread Model B. A decision was made to go ahead with the "BR" in July 1935. Production began in September and simultaneously, an orchard variant of the BR was announced, the "BO."

The BR had only a "service" brake, while the BO received differential brakes. Differential brakes were

soon offered as an option for the BR.

In 1937, the frame of the B-GP was lengthened 5 inches to allow the use of common front-mounted cultivators between the B, the A and the new Model G tractors. This change was incorporated beginning with S/N 42200. Also in 1937, high-clearance versions of the BN and BW were introduced as the BNH and the BWH.

An hydraulic implement lift and electric lighting system were available from the beginning of Model B-GP production, as was a centrally mounted rear PTO and side belt pulley. These first Model Bs are known as "unstyled" by collectors.

During the depression years, only the most doggedly determined farmers survived. They were intensely practical, and not given to frills on their tractors such as mufflers and self-starters, or at least, so it seemed.

By 1935, durable goods manufacturers were employing product styling techniques to differentiate their products from the competition. Some tractor manufacturers were also dressing up their machines. In late 1935, Oliver Hart-Parr brought out the Model 70. It had form and function styling and was an immediate hit. It had a starter, lights, an instrument panel and fingertip controls. It made surprising inroads into Deere's sales of Model A and B tractors.

One of the most respected names in the new industrial design field was Henry Dreyfuss of New York. He and his firm had been involved in improving the looks of products from telephones to kitchen appliances.

Deere and Company sought his consultation for restyling their entire tractor line in 1937. Dreyfuss came to Waterloo, Iowa, in the fall of 1937. Within a month, he had made a wooden mockup of a stylized Model B.

It was more than just a radiator grille. The styling was indeed functional. The grille protected the radiator from field debris. The hood was both striking and slimmer, enhancing visibility of under-mounted cultivators. By late 1938 (for the 1939 model year) newly styled Models A and B tractors were ready for sale. And sell they did! The Model B even more so than the A. From then on, it never fell behind in sales.

Of course, there were some technical improvements. An engine displacement increase to 175 cid from 149 cid was instrumental in increasing torque and enhancing pulling power. Compression was also increased, although distillate was still the fuel of choice.

Options included the hydraulic lift, high- and slow-speed 4-speed transmissions, and 96-inch wheel-tread rear axles on the BN and BW versions. For the 1940 version, a starter and lights were offered, along with some new tire and wheel options.

On tractors with electrical systems, the battery was mounted in an add-on compartment behind the fuel tank. Instruments and the headlight bar were mounted on this compartment, the face of which was tilted forward at the top. Tractors so equipped are now known as "Slant Dash" Bs.

For the 1941 model year, a new 6-speed transmission was available for rubber tire-equipped Bs. Only the 4-speed version was available if steel wheels were ordered. If the special slow-speed transmission was ordered, only

One of only 50 made, this BWH (Model B, Wide front end and High clearance) was especially configured for cultivating corn, cotton and cane.
Keller Collection

The Model BWH-40 was a special version of the Model B, built in 1940. It had high clearance provisions and a wide-front end, making the model designation "BWH." It also had narrow axles to accommodate 40-inch rows. The BWH-40 was extremely rare. Owner: Layher Collection

four speeds were offered, regardless of the wheel and tire choice.

The "slant dash" was now changed to straight vertical, to provide clearance for the new 6-speed shifter. While displacement remained unchanged for 1941, revised combustion chambers and a new DLTX-34 carburetor brought up the horsepower.

No model year changes were subsequently made to the B until after WW II. Changes of convenience and necessity did occur, however. Serial Numbers 136662-166999 had cast iron, rather than steel frames. A pressurized radiator was adopted, then discontinued between S/N 148500-166999. A 1.375 in. diameter PTO spline was adopted at S/N 149700 to conform to ASAE standards. In 1945, the option of "Powr-Trol" hydraulics was offered. This allowed controlling the rockshaft and a remote cylinder.

During the war years, only Model B production was uninterrupted at Deere. Tractor development was continued, since Deere was determined not to be caught napping when the conflict ended.

Standard electric starting, gasoline fuel, improved hydraulics and more power were planned. When the conflict ended in 1945, much of Deere's resources were directed to the new Model M, which was to counter the threat of the extremely popular Ford-Ferguson.

The new "Late-Styled" Model B row crops also were ready for the 1947 model year. The Model M went on to replace the BR and BO (and the H) models.

Electric starting was now standard. The battery was located under a backrest-equipped bench seat. A smart-looking pressed steel frame replaced the stark angle-iron (steel) frame of the previous versions.

An enlarged 190 cid engine, with gasoline or distillate fuel options, was provided. The distillate version was referred to as an "All-Fuel" engine, although its lower compression ratio provided reduced power. Gasoline versions outsold the "All-Fuel" type 10 to one.

The new Powr-Trol hydraulic system was standard, but a regular hydraulic lift could be ordered as a reduced-cost option.

BN and BW tractors were continued, but not the BNH and BWH versions, per se. BN and BW tractors could be ordered with 42-inch rear tires, however. And the BN so ordered would come with a 6.50-16 single front wheel, rather than the 9.00-10 used with 38-inch rears.

BW tractors ordered with 42-inch rear rubber were shipped with extended kingpins to keep the tractor fairly level.

This Model B, Serial Number 1798, was built in December of 1934. It still had the four-bolt front pedestal, which was changed to eight bolts in April of 1935 due to some failures encountered in the field.
Keller Collection

Deere delivered tractors without wheels to Lindeman for the conversion. The one shown was converted in 1945. It also has rubber track pads that allows its owner to drive it on paved areas without causing damage.
Owner: Harold Schultz, Ollie, Iowa

One of the biggest challenges for the Lindeman Brothers in making the conversion was in getting all the control levers handy for the operator, yet not interfering with each other. Some clever angling was required.
Owner: Harold Schultz, Ollie, Iowa.

Overall years built: 1935 – 1952
Overall serial numbers: 1000-310775
Built at: Waterloo, Iowa

Front and rear axle options:

Dual tricycle front/ adjustable splined rear axle(B)

Standard tread (BR) or Orchard configuration (BO)

Adjustable wide front/ adjustable splined rear axle (BW)

Single front wheel/ adjustable splined rear axle (BN)

Adjustable wide front, longer spindles/ longer adjustable splined rear axle (BWH)

Single front wheel / adjustable splined rear axle (BNH)

Crawler (modified BO/ BR)

Industrial (BI)

Wheels/Tires:
1935-1938
Model: B
    Front steel: 22 x 3.25 inch
    Front rubber: 5.00 - 15
    Rear steel: 48 x 5.25 inch
    Rear rubber: 7.50 - 36
             9.00 - 36

Model: BW
    Front steel: 24 x 5 inch
    Front rubber: 5.00 - 15
             5.50 x 15
    Rear steel: 48 x 5.25 inch
    Rear rubber: 7.50 - 36
             9.00 - 36

Model: BN
    Front steel: 22.5 x 8 inch
    Front rubber: 7.50 - 10
             9.00 x 10
    Rear steel: 48 x 5.25 inch
    Rear rubber: 7.50 - 36
             9.00 - 36

Wheels/Tires (cont.):
Model: BNH
    Front steel: N/A
    Front rubber: 6.50 - 16
    Rear steel: N/A
    Rear rubber: 7.50 - 36
             9.00 - 36

Model: BWH
    Front steel: N/A
    Front rubber: 5.00 - 15
    Rear steel: N/A
    Rear rubber: 7.50 - 36
             9.00 - 36

1940-1947
Model: B
    Front rubber: 5.50 - 15
    Rear rubber: 7.50 - 36
             9.00 - 36

Model: BW
    Front rubber: 5.50 - 15
    Rear rubber: 8, 9, 10, or 11 - 38

Model: BN
    Front rubber: 7.50 - 10
             9.00 - 10
    Rear rubber: 8, 9, 10, or 11 - 38

Model: BNH
    Front rubber: 6.50 - 16
    Rear rubber: 7.50 - 40
             9.00 - 40
             11 - 38

Model: BWH
    Front rubber: 5.00 - 15
    Rear rubber: 9.00 - 40
             11 - 38

1947-1952
Model: B
    Front rubber: 5.50 - 16
    Rear rubber: 10 - 38
             11 - 38

1947-1952 cont.

Model: BW
- Front rubber: 5.50 - 16
- Rear rubber: 9 - 42
  - 10 - 38
  - 11 - 38

Model: BN
- Front rubber: 9.00 - 10
  - 7.50 - 16
- Rear rubber: 9 - 42
  - 10 - 38
  - 11 - 38

Model BR, BO:

Front: Steel 24 x 5 in. Rubber – 5.50-16, 5.50 x 15
Rear: Steel 40 x 8 in. Rubber – 9.00 x 28, 10.00 x 28, 11.25 x 24, 11-26
Tread: 41.25 inches, 44.25 with wheels reversed

Serial Numbers:

1000 – 59999 10 spline rear axle (except BWH, BNH with 12 spline axles)
60000- 310772 12 spline rear axles (except BW and BN after 275240, which used 15 spline axles)

Engine Options:

Type: Two-cylinder, four-stroke horizontal, side-by-side with pistons operating in opposition.

1934-1938
- Bore & Stroke: 4.25 x 5.25 in.
- Displacement: 149 cid
- Rated RPM: 1,150

1939-1946
- Bore & Stroke: 4.50 x 5.50 in.
- Displacement: 174.9 cid
- Rated RPM: 1,150

1947-1952
- Bore & Stroke: 4.6875 x 5.50 in.
- Displacement: 190.4 cid
- Rated RPM: 1,250

Carburetors:

All-fuel row crop:
Serial Numbers 1000-95999; Marvel-Schebler DLTX-10
Serial Numbers 96000-200999; Marvel-Schebler DLTX-34
Serial Numbers 201000 and up; Marvel-Schebler DLTX-73

All-fuel standard tread BR, BO, BI:
Serial Numbers 325000 and up Marvel-Schebler DLTX-10

Gasoline:
Serial Numbers 201000 and up Marvel-Schebler DLTX-67

Transmission(standard):

	Gear	Speed (mph)
1935-1940:		
	1	2.33
	2	3.00
	3	4.00
	4	5.25
	Reverse	3.75
1941-1952:		
	1	1.5
	2	2.50
	3	3.50
	4	4.50
	5	5.75
	6	10.00*
	Reverse	2.50

*Tractors prior to S/N 201000 had 6th gear speed of 12.5 mph.

1935-1938:
Model B
- Shipping Weight, lbs.: 3,275
- Length, in.: 120.5
- Height to Radiator, in.: 56
- Price, New: $600-$850

Model BR/BO
- Shipping Weight, lbs.: 3,375
- Length, in.: 117.7
- Height to Radiator, in.: 50.5
- Price, New: $700-$900

1939-1946:

Model B
- Shipping Weight, lbs.: 3,530
- Length, in.: 125.5
- Height to Radiator, in.: 57
- Price, New: $1,000-$1,500

Model BR/BO
- Shipping Weight, lbs.: 3,500
- Length, in.: 117.7
- Height to Radiator, in.: 50.5
- Price, New: $1,000-$2,000

1947-1952:

Model B
- Shipping Weight, lbs.: 4,070
- Length, in.: 132.25
- Height to Radiator, in.: 59.62
- Price, New: $1,650-$2,100

Year Model vs Beginning Serial Number

Year	Serial Number	
1935	1000	B-GP
1936	12012	B-GP
	325000	BO/BR
1937	27389	B-GP
	326655	BO/BR
1938	46175	B-GP
	328111	BO/BR
1939	60000	B-GP
	329000	BO/BR
1940	81600	B-GP
	330633	BO/BR
1941	96000	B-GP
	332039	BO/BR
1942	126345	B-GP
	332427	BO/BR
1943	143420	B-GP
	332780	BO/BR
	332901	Lindeman
1944	152862	B-GP
	333156	BO/BR
	333110	Lindeman
1945	173179	B-GP
	334219	BO/BR
	333666	Lindeman
1946	183673	B-GP
	335641	BO/BR
	335361	Lindeman

Year Model vs Beginning Serial Number cont.

1947	199744	B-GP
	336746	BO/BR
	336441	Lindeman
1948	209295	B-GP
1949	237346	B-GP
1950	258205	B-GP
1951	276557	B-GP
1952	299175	B-GP

Nebraska Test Data

Test Number 232
- Date: 11-1934
- Max. belt. hp.: 15.07
- Max. drawbar pull (lbs.): 1,728
- Specific fuel consumption hp.-hrs./gal.: 10.19
- Weight as tested (lbs.): 3,275

Test Number 305
- Date: 9-1938
- Max. belt. hp.: 18.31
- Max. drawbar pull (lbs.): 2,690
- Specific fuel consumption hp.-hrs./gal.: 10.56
- Weight as tested (lbs.): 3,390

Test Number 366
- Date: 4-1941
- Max. belt. hp.: 19.69
- Max. drawbar pull (lbs.): 2,187
- Specific fuel consumption hp.-hrs./gal.: 11.62
- Weight as tested (lbs.): 4,500

Test Number 380 (gas)
- Date: 5-1947
- Max. belt. hp.: 25.79
- Max. drawbar pull (lbs.): 3,353
- Specific fuel consumption hp.-hrs./gal.: 11.79
- Weight as tested (lbs.): 4,400

Test Number 381 (dist.)
- Date: 5-1947
- Max. belt. hp.: 22.17
- Max. drawbar pull (lbs.): 3,689
- Specific fuel consumption hp.-hrs./gal.: 11.07
- Weight as tested (lbs.): 4,400

Model Variations:
B-GP, BN, BW: 1935-1937, 1000-42199, Short hood, 149 cid engine
B-GP, BN, BW: 1937-1938, 42200-59999, Long hood, 149 cid engine
BNH, BWH: 46175-59999
B-GP, BN, BW, BNH, BWH: 1939-1940, 60000-95999, Styled, 4-speed, 175 cid engine

B-GP, BN, BW, BNH, BWH: 1941-1947, 96000-200999, Styled, 6-speed (S/N 136662-166999 had cast iron frame)
B-GP, BN, BW: 1947-1952, 201000-310775, Late styled, pressed steel frame 190 cid engine
BR, BO: 1935-1938, 325000-328999, 149 cid engine, 4-speed
BR, BO: 1939-1947, 329000-337514, 175 cid, 4-speed

The B was offered, over the years, in four configurations: 1935-1938; unstyled, four-speed transmission, 149-cid engine. 1938-1940: styled, four-speed transmission, 175-cid engine. 1941-1947: styled, six-speed transmission, 175-cid engine. 1947-1952: late-styled (pressed steel frame), six-speed transmission, 190-cid engine.

The late 1930s in the United States were times of slow, painful, but optimistic recovery from bad economic conditions. At the same time, there was an ominous threat of the nation's involvement in military conflict.

In 1937, the progressive farmer was emerging from the Great Depression. He had long since abandoned his horses in favor of a tractor, and was now considering a second larger tractor to get the work done faster. This was the market Deere hoped to penetrate with its new Model G row crop tractor when it was introduced that year.

The new G was a three-plow tractor and had about the same power as the venerable Model D, but was almost 1,000 pounds lighter.

More of the power was available to the drawbar and not so much was used to move the tractor.

Archrival International Harvester had introduced a three-plow row crop machine in 1931 called the F-30, but sales were disappointing, mainly because of the onset of the Great Depression.

At that time, Deere's resources were tied up extensively with the development of their new Models A and B "General Purpose" tractors. They initiated studies of a three-plow machine to be designated the Model F. A, B, GP nee C, and D had been taken for tractors and E was used for a stationary engine.

The "F" designator was carried through several years of gestation, but just before the tractor was released for production, the change was made to Model G. The stated reason was to avoid customer confusion with I-H models like the F-20 and F-30.

Besides three 14-inch plow bottoms, the new G could handle a 28-inch thresher or four-row implements. A four-speed transmission was included with a single lever operating in a cast gate, rather than the two-lever arrangement used on A and B tractors.

A number of optional wheel-tire combinations were offered, including a rare dual rear arrangement with 7.00 x 40 tires. Throughout its life, the G's 412.5-cid engine was meant to burn distillate fuel. Gasoline conversions were offered "after market" that put the G at over 50 hp.

The Model G was the big brother to the Models A and B. It was considered to be a three-plow tractor.

This Hi-Crop version of the Model G is a 1953 version, the last year for the G. All Model Gs were powered by 413-cid all-fuel engines.
Owner: Maurice Horn

The first Model Gs entered the field in May 1937. Soon, complaints began coming in from hot-weather areas that the G was overheating. Deere engineers quickly designed a taller radiator that required a notch in the tank top for the steering shaft to pass though. At Serial Number 4251 tractors left the factory with the new radiator. Deere also offered new radiators to owners of earlier tractors.

Most farmers took the larger radiator, whether or not they were experiencing overheating. Old short, or "low," radiators were generally scrapped. Today, an original early G with an authentic low radiator is the Holy Grail of many collectors of antique Deere tractors. There were some other modifications to the engine, water pipes and radiator shutters to also enhance cooling.

In 1939, after only a few more than 7,000 Gs had been built, International Harvester brought out its line of tractors styled by designer Raymond Loewy. The "F" designation was dropped in favor of single letters A, B, H and M. The M replaced the F-30 and was a direct

competitor to Deere's Model G. By comparison, the unstyled G looked a little shabby next to the new bright red M. Deere had Dreyfuss-styled competitors for the other models, but the G was to remain unstyled until the 1942 model year, a fact that hurt its sales.

The 1942 styled G was as handsome a tractor as could be found anywhere. While the engine remained the same, a new six-speed transmission was provided. New options included an electrical system with a starter and lights.

The styled G cost more to build, so Deere applied to the War Production Board (WPB) for permission to raise the price. The function of the WPB was to prevent wartime price increases, so the request was denied.

At Ford in Dearborn, Henry Ford had run into the same problem with his 9N tractor. Ford solved the problem by announcing a new model, the 2N. It was essentially the same as the 9N, but with minor improvements and the elimination of some war-critical materials.

A price increase was granted by the WPB for new models. So Deere immediately followed suit, renaming the styled G the GM (for modernized) and also received an OK to raise the price.

When WPB restrictions were lifted in 1946, the GM reverted to just plain G. The actual change took place in early 1947 at serial Number 23000. The main difference between the GM and the new G was in the serial number prefix (G rather than GM). Roll-O-Matic front axles were now an option.

Within two months of the reversion to the G designation, two new front-end options were added. The first was a single front wheel version called the GN, the second was a wide front (GW), both with optional 104-inch rear tread axles. These front-end options were occasioned by the advent of a split pedestal of the same type that had been used on the Models A and B.

In July 1947, another jump to an even serial number

(S/N 26000) was made. The G was being brought up, more-or-less, to the "Late-Styled" standards of the Models A and B. The most obvious difference was the change from the pan seat to the bench seat with backrest. The model identifier letter was moved from the seat strut to the hood sides like the others in the line. Electric starting now became standard equipment. Other improvements, such as the Powr-Trol hydraulic system, were added over the next years, and in 1951, at S/N 46894, a Hi-Crop (GH) were added. In 1952, the thermosyphon cooling system (which worked with gravity and the density of hot versus cold water) was replaced by a system with a water pump.

Towards the end of its production life, the G was selling so well that it was continued into the 1953 model year, months after production of it's A and B row crop siblings had stopped. Then, the mighty Model 70 picked up where the G left off.

Overall years built: 1937 – 1953
Overall serial numbers: 1000-64530
Built at: Waterloo, Iowa

Front and rear axle options: Dual tricycle
front/ adjustable splined rear axle (G), (GM)
Adjustable wide front/ adjustable splined rear
axle (GW- Styled, only)
Single front wheel / Adjustable splined rear axle
(GN-Styled, only)
Adjustable wide front, longer spindles/
adjustable splined rear axle with drop boxes
(GH-Styled, only and 1951-1953, only)

Wheels/Tires:
1937-1941
Model: G
Front steel: 24.5 x 5 inch
Front rubber: 6.00 - 16
Rear steel: 51.5 x 7 inch
Rear rubber: 10/11.25 - 36
Dual 7.00 - 40

1942-1953
Model: G
Front steel: 24 x 5 inch
Front rubber: 6.00 - 16
Rear steel: 51.5 x 7 inch
Rear rubber: 12/13 - 38

Model: GW
Front steel: 24 x 5 inch
Front rubber: 6.00 - 16
Rear steel: 51.5 x 7 inch
Rear rubber: 12/13 - 38

Model: GN
Front steel: 24 x 5 inch
Front rubber: 6.00 - 16
Rear steel: 51.5 x 7 inch
Rear rubber: 12/13 - 38

Model: GH
Front steel: N/A
Front rubber: 7.50 - 16
Rear steel: N/A
Rear rubber: 12/13 - 38

Wheels/Tires (cont.):
Model: GM
Front steel: 24 x 5 inch
Front rubber: 6.00 - 16
Rear steel: 51.5 x 7 inch
Rear rubber: 12/13 - 38

Engine:
Type: Two-cylinder, four-stroke, horizontal side-
by-side with pistons operating in opposition,
overhead valves.

1937-1953
Bore & Stroke: 6.125 x 7.00 in.
Displacement: 412.5 cid
Rated RPM: 975 rpm
Compression Ratio: 4.20:1

G-Row Crop:
1937-1941
Weight: 4,488 lbs.
Height (to top of hood): 61.5 in.
Length: 135 in.
Price, new: $1,185

1942-1953
Weight: 5,624 lbs.
Height (to top of hood): 65.87 in.
Length: 137.5 in.
Price, new: $2,600

Transmission:

	Gear	Speed (mph)
1937-1941:		
	1	2.25
	2	3.25
	3	4.25
	4	6.00
	Reverse	3.00
1942-1953:		
	1	2.50
	2	3.50
	3	4.50
	4	6.50
	5	8.75
	6	12.50
	Reverse	3.50

Year Model vs Beginning Serial Number

Model Unstyled G

Year	Beginning Serial Number	Notes
1937	1000	2150-2199 not used
1938	2601	7001-7099 not used
1939	7100	8900-9199 not used
1940	9200	
1941	10141	
1942	11561	

Model GM

Year	Beginning Serial Number	Notes
1942	13000	13747 last built due to WWII
1943	None	
1944	13748	
1945	13905	
1946	16694	
1947	18553	22112 last GM

Model New G

Year	Beginning Serial Number	Notes
1947	23000	
1948	25235	
1949	32457	
1950	39161	
1951	46809	
1952	53479	
1953	63138	64530 last

Nebraska Test Data

Test Number 295
Date: 11-1937
Max. belt. hp.: 34.09
Max. drawbar pull (lbs.): 4,085
Specific fuel consumption hp.-hrs./gal.: 10.59
Weight as tested (lbs.): 4,400

Test Number 383
Date: 6-1947
Max. belt. hp.: 36.03
Max. drawbar pull (lbs.): 4,394
Specific fuel consumption hp.-hrs./gal.: 10.74
Weight as tested (lbs.): 6,065

The G could also handle a 28-inch thresher or four-row cultivating implements. Styled Gs had six-speed transmissions, while unstyled Gs used a four-speed unit.

Model H

"To meet the demands of small-acreage farmers everywhere for a tractor that will handle all power jobs at rock-bottom cost, and meet the demands of large-acreage farmers who have always wanted and needed economical auxiliary power to handle lighter farm jobs, John Deere offers the new one-two plow Model H."

Thus reads the 1939 sales brochure introducing the new John Deere Model H.

Well into the 1940s, Deere sales people were still trying to talk the small farmer out of his horses, and at the same time, were selling a small tractor to go along with big ones for the large farms.

The small farmer was the biggest untapped market. While economics proved one tractor could do the work of several teams, the initial cost of a tractor was the problem. If the farmer could be talked into selling all of his horses he would have the price of a basic Model H.

The Model H was built along the classic all-purpose lines, able to replace all of the horses on a farm of less than 80 acres.

The Deere marketing department put out the following goals to engineering when defining the Model H in 1937.

- Lower the purchase price through simplified design, improved materials and reduced parts count.
- Lower operating cost through balancing of engine power with the anticipated job, the use of low-cost distillate fuels, and reduced power losses as a result of lightweight construction and the use of large diameter rubber tires.

The Model H was a small tractor designed to follow the lines of the successful Models A and B. It was aimed at the small farmer still using one or two teams of horses.
Owners: Ray Mesecher and Marty Brackin, Hazelhurst, Wisconsin

The wide and high version of the H, this 1941 example, like most John Deere 126 HWHs, was used in the truck gardens of the Sacramento, California area.
Owner: Keller Collection

• Improve adaptability through adjustable wheel spacing.

By 1937, prototypes were available for testing designated OX138 to OX143. Some of these were basic tractors, but later ones had rudimentary styled sheet metal. The H was ready for production for the 1939 model year, and the OX prototypes were scrapped.

As a cost-saving measure, the H engine, a typical John Deere side-by-side horizontal two-cylinder, provided its power output from the camshaft instead of the crankshaft. Since the camshaft operates at half the crankshaft speed, expensive bull gears in the final drive were not required.

It also meant that a reasonably-sized belt pulley could be used without reduction gearing. To save the cost of a road gear, a governor over-ride gas pedal was added. In third-gear, 1800 rpm was available, rather than the rated 1400 rpm that gave about two-miles-per-

hour more speed.

The appearance of the Ford-Ferguson 9N in mid-1939 caught Deere, Inc. by surprise. By the 1941 model year, they were able to sweeten their offering with a "live" hydraulic system, capable of operating two remote cylinders, and with a self-starter (beginning with S/N 27000).

While the little Ford had a major impact on the future of the tractor industry and sold extremely well, it was no match for the Model H regarding versatility. The H had easily adjustable rear wheels and was available in high-clearance versions.

The H had front-mounted cultivators with the ability to handle up to eight rows. The 9N was relegated to rear three-point cultivators. Although rear cultivators eventually became the norm, they encountered stiff resistance in early going.

Model H

Data and Specifications

Overall Years Built: 1939-1947
Overall Serial Numbers: 1000-61116
Built At: Waterloo

Front and Rear Axle Options:
Row Crop, Dual Tricycle Front (H)
Row Crop, Single Front Wheel (HN)
Row Crop, Adjustable Wide-front (HW)
Row Crop, Single Front Wheel, High Clearance (HNH)
Row Crop, Adjustable Wide-front, High Clearance (HWH)

Wheels/Tires:
Model: H
    Front: 4.00 - 15
    Rear: 7.50 - 32

Model: HN
    Front: 6.00 - 12
    Rear: 7.50 - 32

Model: HW
    Rear: 7.50 - 32

Model: HNH
    Front: 6.00 - 12
    Rear: 8.00 - 38

Model: HWH
    Rear: 8.00 - 38

Engine Options:
    Bore & Stroke: 3.5625 x 5.00
    Displacement: 99.7cid
    Rated RPM: 1400
    Fuel: Distillate
    Ignition: Magneto
    Cooling: Thermosyphon

Transmission(standard):

Gear	Speed (mph)
1	2.5
2	3.5
3	5.75*
Reverse	1.75

*Using foot-throttle governor override, top speed is 7.5 mph @ 1800 rpm.

Shipping weight: 3,035 lbs.

Length: 112.5 in.

Height to radiator: 52.5 in.

Width/ wheel tread variation: 44 to 88 in.

Price, New: $595 – 650

Model Variations:

Designation	Total Produced
H	57,450
HN	978
HNH	37
HWH	126
Total	58,591

Nebraska Test Data
Tractor Tested: John Deere H (dist.)
Test Number 312
Date: 11-1938
Max. belt. hp.: 14.22
Max. drawbar pull (lbs.): 1,839
Specific fuel consumption hp.-hrs./gal.: 11.95
Weight as tested (lbs.): 3,035

Year Model vs. Beginning Serial Number

Year	Beginning Serial Number
1939	1000
1940	10000
1941	20615
1942	35699
1943	44754
1944	45642
1945	47796
1946	53327
1947	58614

This 1941 John Deere Model HWH has an electric starter, a hydraulic lift and an extra wide front axle.
Owner: Keller Collection

The small, inexpensive tractor has always been the nemesis of the tractor maker. Just as with the small, cheap car, the goal of "inexpensive" proves to be illusive. So much of the cost is not reduced in proportion to size, and customers resist products that appear to be tawdry.

Many 1920s-era tractor makers (including Deere) tried to make motor cultivators, but without success. Costs seemed always to be prohibitive in lieu of the machine's productivity.

International Harvester's Farmall grew out of motor cultivator studies, but it came out at about 20 hp and nearly $1,000.

The Farmall replaced three teams of horses, not just one!

Studies in the early '30s indicated 60 percent of American farms were one- or two-team farms. At that time, a team of horses could be purchased for $100 to $500, depending on their size, type, age, condition, etc.

The $500 amount was considered the upper limit for a tractor that would do what a team could do. Naturally, the tractor didn't get tired or slow down on a hot day, nor did a tractor "eat" when not working.

Tractor makers had evidence from previous activities that a $500 tractor would sell, if it could do the job and not cause too much trouble. Examples were the 1913 Bull tractor that sold for $335, and the 1922 Fordson, which sold for $395. Neither was financially successful at those prices, but they did sell.

Deere's foray into the $500 tractor market began in

In 1935, Deere began working the Model Y, an inexpensive tractor to replace a team of horses. That effort influenced the improved Deere Model 62 in 1936. Dual foot brakes were provided. The steering wheel and shaft were supported by a pylon strut mounted to the rear axle.
Owner: Keller Collection

Deere began making the engine, instead of using one made by Hercules. The Deere engine had provisions for an electric starter. These small John Deeres were made in the Moline (Illinois) Wagon Works.
Owner: Keller Collection

The Model L was quite different from other Deere tractors in that it used a vertical two-cylinder gasoline-only engine and a foot-operated clutch. The one shown is the first L off the assembly line in 1937. It is Serial Number 621079.
Owner: Keller Collection

1935 in the depths of the Great Depression. Engineer Willard Nordensen and four teammates were given the directive to "…make a small tractor, but don't spend any money at it."

The Moline Wagon Works production was declining, due to the Depression and to reduced demand for wooden wagons. So Nordensen set up shop in the Wagon Works building.

Part of what had prompted interest in the small tractor at that time was the availability of a small, vertical, two-cylinder engine from the Novo company. The side-valve engine resembled half of a Model A Ford engine. The Novo was designed to be a stationary power plant and later proved to have inadequate lubrication for tractor duty.

The John Deere small tractor, initially dubbed the Model Y, was designed around the little Novo engine, which, strangely, mated well with a Ford Model A three-speed transmission. A Model A Ford steering

post, wheel, steering gearbox and throttle lever were also used.

The use of readily available Ford parts greatly reduced development time and costs. A sturdy tubing frame was fabricated. The little tractor had left and right hand brakes, and an industrial tractor type seat.

About 24 of these Model Y tractors, with either the Novo engine, or later, with a similar Hercules engine, were built for testing. About a year later, all were supposedly returned to the factory and destroyed. The lessons learned were to be incorporated into a redesign known as the Model 62.

Several enterprising collectors have built Model Y replicas from extant photographs, but otherwise, none are known to exist.

The success of the Model Y prototypes convinced Deere management to approve a budget for further development of the small tractor. This version was to be called the Model 62. Work began on it in 1936.

The LA came out in 1941 as a more powerful version of the Model L using a 76-cid vertical two-cylinder engine that produce 14 belt hp (up from 10 on the L). It was also heavier at 2,200 lbs., up from 1,550 lbs.

The Hercules engine was to be retained, but a Spicer transmission was used. It was mounted directly to the differential. This configuration resulted in an engine-speed drive shaft connecting the engine to the transmission.

Besides the obvious weight distribution advantages, a bevel-gear-driven belt pulley could be placed between the engine and transmission on the left side of the tractor. A similar tubing frame was retained, but the backrest seat was replaced with a pressed-steel pan seat.

Dual foot brakes were provided. The Model A steering post and wheel were also gone, replaced by a wheel and shaft supported by a pylon strut mounted to the rear axle.

It is believed 78 Model 62s were built in 1937 with 72 shipped to customers and six retained by the factory. There is some confusion about the first Model 62 serial number being 621000, or 621001. Records are clear the last model 62 was 621078.

The $500 target price for the Model 62 proved difficult to achieve, so some redesign was required. The expensive cast wheels were replaced by pressed steel types. The fancy "JD" logos on the "chin" and rear axle were eliminated. The fenders also were trimmed.

In September 1937, the revised Model 62 became the Model L (a designation more in keeping with those used on the Waterloo tractors). The same serial number system was used, so the first Model L was S/N 621079.

A host of Deere-designed implements were quickly provided for the L, but many horse-type implements could be modified for use with the little tractor. Production records no longer exist, so the exact number of "unstyled" Model Ls isn't known for certain. Between 1,300 and 1,500 were built, and some experts put the number at 1,502.

During the 1939 model year and beginning with S/N 625000, the Model L received Dreyfuss styling and the Hercules NXB engine in which the bore diameter was increased to 3.25 inches. Beginning with S/N 640000, a Deere-built engine replaced the Hercules.

This engine was much the same and most parts are interchangeable. The Deere version has a one-piece casting for the block and clutch housing. Also, the Deere engine has provisions for a starter and generator.

The final version of the "Baby Deere" was the Model LA. Introduced in 1941, the LA was produced simultaneously with the L. The LA had its own serial number sequence, starting with S/N 1001 and a more powerful Deere-built engine with a 3.5-inch bore.

It was larger and heavier and cost about $60 more than the L. The LA also offered a rear 540 rpm PTO.

Model 62

Years built: March - July, 1937
Built at: Moline, Illinois
Number built: 78
Configuration: Utility

Wheels/Tires:
   Front: 4.00 x 15
   Rear: 6.00 x 22

Engine: Hercules NXA 2-cyl.
Fuel: gasoline
   Bore/stroke: 3.0 x 4.0 in.
   Displacement: 56.5 cid
   Rated rpm: 1,550
   Ignition: magneto
   Cooling: thermosyphon
Transmission: 3-speed transaxle
Speeds: 2.5, 3.75, 6 mph
Reverse: 2.5 mph
Shipping weight: 1,500 lbs.
Length: 91 in.
Height to radiator: 57 in.
Price, new: $450

Model L

Years built: Sept. 1937-1946
Built at: Moline, Illinois
Number built: (see text)
Configuration: Utility

Wheels/Tires:
   Front: 5.00 x 15
   Rear: 7.50 x 22

Engine: (see below)
   Fuel: gasoline
   Bore/stroke: (see below)
   Displacement: (see below)
   Rated rpm: 1,550
   Ignition: magneto
   Cooling: thermosyphon
Transmission: 3-speed transaxle
Speeds: 2.5, 3.75, 6 mph
Reverse: 2.5 mph
Shipping weight: 1,550-1,570 lbs.
Length: 91 in.
Height to radiator: 57 in.
Price, new: $475-$520

Model LA

Years built: 1941-1946
Built at: Moline, Illinois
Number built: 12,500+
Configuration: Utility

Wheels/Tires:
   Front: 5.00 x 15
   Rear: 9.00 x 24

Engine: Deere 2-cyl.
   Fuel: gasoline
   Bore/stroke: 3.50 x 4.0 in.
   Displacement: 77 cid
   Rated rpm: 1,850
   Ignition: magneto or
   distributor
   Cooling: thermosyphon
Transmission: 3-speed transaxle
Speeds: 2.5, 3.75, 9 mph
Reverse: 2.5 mph
Shipping weight: 2,200 lbs.
Length: 93 in.
Height to radiator: 60 in.
Price, new: $575-$600

The Hercules engine was retained on the John Deere Model 62, but the transmission was now mounted directly to the differential, rather than to the engine. A drive shaft connecting the engine to the transmission. Owner: Keller Collection

Model L Engine Variations

1936 to 1938 were "unstyled" with Hercules NXA 56.5-cid, two-cylinder engines (S/N 621079 to S/N 622580).
Bore and stroke were 3.0 x 4.0 inches.
1938 to 1941 were "styled" with Hercules NXB 66.4-cid, two-cylinder engines (S/N 62500 to S/N 634840).
Bore and stroke were 3.25 x 4.0 inches.
1941 to 1946 were "styled" with Deere 66.4 cid, two-cylinder engines (S/N 640000 to S/N 642038).
Bore and stroke were 3.25 x 4.0 inches.

Nebraska Test Data

Model L
Test Number 313
Date: 11-1938
Max. belt. hp.: 10.42
Max. drawbar pull (lbs.): 1,235
Specific fuel consumption hp.-hrs./gal.: 9.82
Weight as tested (lbs.): 2,180

Model LA
Test Number 373
Date: 6-1941
Max. belt. hp.: 14.34
Max. drawbar pull (lbs.): 1,936
Specific fuel consumption hp.-hrs./gal.: 10.47
Weight as tested (lbs.): 3,490

Model 62, L Serial Number vs. Year Model

Year	Beginning Serial Number
1937	621001 (Model 62)
1938	621079 (622581 last unstyled L, 625000 First styled L)
1939	626265
1940	630160
1941	634191
1942	640000
1943	640738
1944	641038
1945	641538
1946	941938 (642038 Last Styled L)

Model LA

Year	Beginning Serial Number
1941	1001
1942	5361
1943	6029
1944	6159
1945	9732
1946	11529 (13475 Last Model LA

First produced in 1937, the L was designed to replace a team of horses. Its layout was unique for its time with the driver's seat offset to the right.
Owner: Keller Collection

In the 1920s and 1930s, John Deere engineers and management saw their tractor competition not so much from other implement companies as from the horse. The challenge was to make a tractor for the farmer that could do what the horses of a given size farm could do.

On the large end of the scale, the mighty models D and G replaced many teams of horses. At the other end, the Deere models L, LA and H were made for the small farms with one or two teams to replace.

The year 1939 saw Henry Ford back in the tractor business with his Model 9N. Ford had collaborated with the Irishman Harry Ferguson and incorporated Ferguson's three-point hydraulic implement system into the 2,500-lb. tractor. The Ford-Ferguson tractor

had been under development for less than a year when it was introduced to the public in October with great fanfare typical of Harry Ferguson's ebullient marketing style. Deere, and other tractor makers, were taken by surprise, but weren't too worried.

They had competed with Ford before, on the Fordson tractor, from 1918 to 1927. Ford had sold a lot of tractors in that time, but mostly at prices that cost him money. The Fordson whetted the farmers' appetites for power farming, getting many of them into the game who otherwise would have had to stick with their horses.

The Fordson also prompted the major tractor makers to build more useful tractors that justified a higher (and more profitable) price with the advent of the "general

The Deere Model M was designed to replace the Models L, LA, BR, BO and H. It was Deere's first true "utility"-configuration tractor (the utility was to be a combination row-crop and standard-tread machine).
Owner: Bob Pollock Collection

purpose" machines, such as the John Deere Models GP, A and B.

The new Ford-Ferguson 9N tractor sold very well at its $585 introductory price despite the fact the farmer had to buy new implements to gain the advantages offered by the Ferguson three-point system.

More than 10,000 of the little gray machines rolled into the fields in the remaining three months of 1939. Deere management was quick to acquire examples of Ford's offering for in-house tests. They found while the 9N could do a great job of plowing, but lacked traction to do much else without the weight transfer effect of an implement, or much ballast, on the back wheels.

The most intriguing thing was its handiness. Implements could be changed in minutes. With the driver's seat forward, it was much easier to mount and dismount than conventional platform tractors. It started, sounded and drove much like a small car.

Deere's Waterloo Tractor Works had pioneered hydraulics as far back as 1934, so going to the three-point system wasn't a technical problem, but Ferguson had it tied up in patents. Then, World War II intervened

and only existing tractor designs could be sold.

The John Deere Moline Tractor Works went ahead with design studies. By 1943, a completely new small tractor, designated the Model 69, was on paper. In keeping with tradition, the drawings showed a two-cylinder engine.

The Model 69 design borrowed from both previous Deere tractors, and from the competition. It would be about the size and power of the Deere Model H, but it would have a vertical "in-line" engine like the Model L. It would be "frameless" like the Ford and others such as the Allis Chalmers Model B. All these tractors relied on the cast iron engine and transmission housings to act as a frame.

By 1944, a prototype Model 69 was ready for testing. By late 1944, a three-point hydraulic lift system was ready to be incorporated. It had been developed by the "Quick-Tatch Committee," made up of engineers from both the Moline and Waterloo factories and implement factories. The hydraulic control system was named the "Touch-O-Matic," but nicknamed the "Liquid Brain."

The new system did mostly what the Ferguson

The M used a high-speed (for Deere) vertical two-cylinder with a 4-in. bore and stroke for a displacement of 100.5 cid coupled to a four-speed gearbox. Power was 21 belt hp at 1,650 rpm.
Owner: Bob Pollock Collection

Deere purchased the Lindeman Company in 1946, so the MC, sold from 1949 to 1952, was the first all-Deere crawler. Tractor units, sans wheels, were shipped to Yakima, Washington to be fitted with tracks. Track assemblies also were shipped to the new Deere factory in Dubuque to be mated with tractors for the rest of the country.
Owners: Bob Pollock/Tony Dieter Collection

system did, but with easier implement attachment. The one drawback was in the area of depth control, which Ferguson's patents protected. The Deere system was mechanical and somewhat crude compared to Ferguson's draft load-controlled hydraulic arrangement, but it worked reasonably well. In fact, tractors without depth control (and many on which it isn't working), plow reasonably well with the operator working the hydraulic lever manually.

In January of 1945, Deere acquired 730 acres of land near Dubuque, Iowa, for a new tractor plant. The new tractor, now called the Model M (in keeping with the other letter-series tractors) was to be built there when the war ended. Delays in acquiring materials for the new plant due to shortages caused the build date to slip to March 1947.

Production of the Models L, LA, H, BR and BO was terminated in 1946 and 1947. Deere counted on the new M to replace all of these units.

Since the BO had found considerable success as a crawler, modified to that configuration by the Lindeman Brothers of Yakima, Washington, a Model M, less wheels,

etc., was shipped to the Lindeman operation in 1947. The results were so encouraging that Deere bought out the Lindeman Brothers and took over their operation. Crawler development continued both at Yakima and the Moline test farm.

The other variation of the M was the MT (for Tricycle). It was a two-row crop tractor that could be ordered in dual tricycle, single wheel, or wide-front row crop configurations. It was much the same as the regular M except it was built to provide more clearance for tall crops. A new split rockshaft implement lift allowed separate control of forward and aft cultivators and was available on the MT. Both the MT and the MC went into production in 1948.

Unique features of the M and MT include a telescoping steering column. Henry Dreyfuss was much involved in the layout of the tractor and insisted that the operator must be able to stand while driving.

This required either a seat or a steering wheel that could be moved. Apparently, the moveable wheel was chosen. Another feature, also attributed to Dreyfuss, was the backrest seat with an air-bladder seat cushion.

Model M ◆◆ 73

Model M
Data and Specifications

Overall Years Built: 1947-1952	**Serial Numbers:** 10001-50580	**Built at:** Dubuque, Iowa

Model M

Years built: 1947-1952
Built at: Dubuque, Iowa
Number built: 45,799
Configuration: Utility

Wheels/Tires:
   Front: 4.00 x 15/5.00 x 15
   Rear: 8, 9 or 10 - 24

Transmission: 4-speed
Speeds: 1.63, 3.13, 4.25, 10.0
   mph (9-24 rears)
Reverse: 1.63 mph
Shipping weight: 2,695 lbs.
Price, new: $1,100

Model MT

Years built: 1949-1952
Built at: Dubuque, Iowa
Number built: 30,472
Configuration: Row Crop

Wheels/Tires:
   Front: 5.00 x 15
   Rear: 9 - 34

Transmission: 4-speed
Speeds: 1.75, 3.25, 4.50, 11.0
   mph
Reverse: 1.75 mph
Shipping weight: 3,183 lbs.
Price, new: $1,200

Model MC

Years built: 1949-1952
Built at: Dubuque, Iowa
Number built: 10,509
Configuration: Crawler

Wheels/Tires/Tracks:
   Front: 10, 12 or 14 in. track shoes
   Rear: 3-roller undercarriage

Transmission: 4-speed
Speeds: 0.96, 2.20, 2.90, 4.70 mph
Reverse: 1.00 mph
Shipping weight: 4,293 lbs.

Engine Options:
Bore & stroke: 4.00 x 4.00 inches, two cylinders
Displacement: 100.54 cid
Rated RPM: 1650
Fuel: gasoline*

Compression ratio: 6:1
Ignition: coil*
Cooling: thermosyphon

*Some Model Ms may have been built with all-fuel systems and/or with magneto ignition systems, but these are rare, indeed.

Competitor Comparisons:

Name	Engine	Max. hp.	SFC*	Max. DB pull, lbs.	Test wt., lbs.
John Deere MT	101 cid, 2-cyl	19.8	11.16	2,385	3,869
Case VAC	124 cid, 4-cyl	20.06	10.74	2,768	4,183
Allis B	125 cid, 4-cyl	21.17	11.45	2,667	4,001
Farmall A	113 cid, 4cyl	16.86	11.97	2,387	3,570
Ford 8N	120 cid, 4-cyl	25.49	11.18	2,810	4,043

*Specific Fuel Consumption in horsepower-hours per gallon.

Serial Numbers vs. Year Model

Serial Numbers	Year
Model M	
10001-13733	1947
13734-25603	1948
25604-35658	1949
35659-43524	1950
43525-50579	1951
50580-55799	1952
Model MT	
10001-14727	1949
14728-25272	1950
25273-32812	1951
32813-40472	1952
Model MC	
10001-11092	1949
11093-13373	1950
13374-15340	1951
15341-20509	1952

Nebraska Test Data

Model M
Test Number 387
Date: 10-1947
Max. belt. hp.: 19.49
Max. drawbar pull (lbs.): 2,329
Specific fuel consumption hp.-hrs./gal.: 11.12
Weight as tested (lbs.): 3,495

Model MT
Test Number 423
Date: 9-1949
Max. belt. hp.: 19.8
Max. drawbar pull (lbs.): 2,385
Specific fuel consumption hp.-hrs./gal.: 11.16
Weight as tested (lbs.): 3,869

Model MC
Test Number 448
Date: 7-1950
Max. belt. hp.: 20.12
Max. drawbar pull (lbs.): 4,226
Specific fuel consumption hp.-hrs./gal.: 11.36
Weight as tested (lbs.): 4,293

Standard equipment included an oil bath air cleaner, a Marvel-Schebler carburetor, plus an electrical system with a starter. Optional equipment included the new Touch-O-Matic hydraulic lift.
Owner: Bob Pollock Collection

John Deere Model 40

Edsel Ford, Henry Ford's only son, died in 1943. At the time of his death, he was president of Ford Motor Company, a company wholly owned by the Ford family. Henry Ford, despite his advancing age and slight mental debilitation due to a series of minor strokes, was again pressed into day-to-day management of the giant firm.

Since Ford Motor Company had war production contracts of immense importance to the war effort, it would be an understatement to say government officials were quite worried about the situation. Henry Ford II, Edsel's oldest son and grandson of Henry, was released from the U.S. Navy so he could become involved in company management. Henry II was just 26-years-old at the time.

A bitter struggle ensued among several top Ford management personnel as they jockeyed to replace the aging auto magnate. The struggle soon reached a fever pitch. Old Henry indicated he favored Harry Bennett, but Ford's wife, Clara, and Eleanor Ford, Edsel's widow, threatened to vote their stock shares against Henry unless he named his grandson, Henry II, to the top post.

Old Henry caved in to their pressure, and in 1945 as World War II ended, Young Henry (as he came to be called) became president and chief executive officer. His first official act was to fire Harry Bennett.

Young Henry's next official act was to get an accounting of the company's financial status. He learned the tractor operation (which sold tractors only to Harry Ferguson, Inc.) had never made the company any profit.

The Model 40 replaced the M in 1953. Engine power was up by about 15 percent because the operating speed was increased from 1,650rpm to 1,850rpm.
Owner: Keller Collection

The Hi-Crop version came out in 1954 and offered a crop clearance of 26.5-inches.
Owner: Keller Collection

Ferguson, who had borrowed money from Ford to get started retailing tractors and implements, had become a multi-millionaire. In September 1946, The Ford Motor Company announced dissolution of its agreement with Harry Ferguson. (It had been a provision of the famous "handshake agreement" between Ford and Ferguson that either could end the relationship at any time, without explanation.)

Ending the relationship did not bother Ferguson, as he had already started building his own version of the tractor in England. When Ford announced a new and improved version, the 8N, Ferguson sued for patent infringement (mainly for the hydraulic three-point lift system).

The $251 million suit was settled out of court in 1952 for a little over $9 million. The settlement cleared up the situation concerning the patents held by Ferguson for the system. Now Ford and others could use the system.

Deere lost no time in adapting the three-point hitch with hydraulic control to an improved version of the Model M, scheduled for release in 1953. It was identified as the Model MA (or MTA, etc.). The decision to change to numbered tractor identifiers in early 1952, however, caused the M series to become the 40 series.

The new Model 40 retained much of the M's configuration. The engine was beefed up and given a higher compression ratio (6.5:1 rather than 6.0:1). For the Model 40, the rated operating speed would be raised from 1650 rpm to 1850 rpm giving it about 15 percent more horsepower. The four-speed transmission was retained. Besides the standard (S), the row crop (T) and the crawler (C) versions of the M, four additional versions of the 40 were offered.

40S Standard:

The 40S Standard was introduced in November 1952 and featured a one-piece fluted grille, fixed- width wide front axle and an improved operator's station. Gone were the telescoping steering column and bladder seat, replaced by a sliding seat with a conventional cushion and armrests and an adjustable backrest.

40T Row Crop:

The 40T Row Crop was introduced in November 1952, and was available with dual narrow front end, single front wheel, or adjustable wide front. The grille was split in two pieces in order to provide mounting

The Hi-Crop version came out in 1954 and offered a crop clearance of 26.5-inches.
Owner: Keller Collection

points for front mounted cultivators, etc. The T was higher than the S, due to longer kingpins and larger rear tires, to provide more crop clearance. Operator station improvements were applicable to all versions.

40C Crawler:

The 40C Crawler had the same one-piece grille as the Standard. Initially, a three-roller undercarriage frame of Lindeman design was used. After Serial Number 62263, four or five roller frames, made in Dubuque, Iowa, were used. These greatly improved the stability and handling of the crawler, and eliminated track-throwing problems.

40U Utility:

The 40U Utility came out in the 1954 model year as a direct competitor to Ford, which had pioneered the "utility" configuration. A "utility" tractor is one that is low enough for grove work, but retains enough clearance for crop work. It is also suitable for industrial uses, highway mowing and working a front loader attachment. Wheel tread widths are adjustable. Most tractor manufacturers offered utility tractors beginning in 1954, along with a draft-controlled three-point hitch.

The John Deere 40U was lower than the Standard by 8 inches. This was accomplished by rotating the final drive gearbox 90 degrees aft. The front kingpins were also shortened by 8 inches.

40V Special:

The 40V Special was introduced in the final year of Model 40 production (1955), the 40V was based on the 40S Standard. It used 34-inch rear wheels and longer kingpins to get 26 inches of crop clearance. The 40V proved to be ideal for vegetable growers.

40H Hi-Crop:

The 40H Hi-Crop also was introduced in 1955. The 40H was 10 inches longer than the Standard. A 10-inch plug, or spacer, was installed between the engine and transmission to increase longitudinal stability when using 3-point hitch implements. It offered 32 inches of crop clearance, and unlike the 40V, it could handle cultivation of two rows, instead of just one.

40W Two-Row Utility:

The 40W Two-Row Utility also made its debut in 1955. The 40W was taller than the "U" through the use of 10-34 (or 12-28) tires and wheels, and it was also capable of wider tread widths for two-row cultivation.

Options for the 40 series included the oval muffler that was standard on later models, a cigarette lighter on the dashboard, an hour meter, an underneath exhaust, remote hydraulic system, and power adjustable rear wheel spacing (identified by silver-painted wheels).

All versions of the Model 40 had their own serial numbering system beginning at 60001.

The 40 Series tractors had an optional three-point hitch with load and depth control and dual rockshafts for mounted implements. This version has dual lifts but no three-point hitch.
Owner: Keller Collection

The driver's view from the Model 40. This is Serial Number 60001, the first Model 40 Hi-Crop built.
Owner: Keller Collection

Model 40
Data and Specifications

Overall Years Built: 1953-1955

Model 40S
Years built: 1953-1955
Built at: Dubuque, Iowa
Number built: 11,814
Configuration: Standard Tread

Wheels/Tires:
   Front: 5.00 x 15/6.00 x 16
   Rear: 9, 10 or 11 - 24

Transmission: 4-speed
Speeds: 1.63, 3.13, 4.25,
   12.0 mph
Reverse: 2.50 mph
Shipping weight: 2,750 lbs.
Price, new: $1,521

Model 40U
Years built: 1953-1955
Built at: Dubuque, Iowa
Number built: 5,208
Configuration: Utility

Wheels/Tires:
   Front: 5.00 x 15/6.00 x 16
   Rear: 10 - 24 or 11-24
       11 - 26 to 13-26

Transmission: 4-speed
Speeds: 1.63, 3.13, 4.25,
   12.0 mph
Reverse: 2.50 mph
Shipping weight: 2,850 lbs.
Price, new: $1,541

Model 40W
Years built: 1955
Built at: Dubuque, Iowa
Number built: 1,758
Configuration: Wide 2-row
   Utility

Wheels/Tires:
   Front: 5.00 x 15/6.00 x 16
   Rear: 9 - 34 or 10 - 34

Transmission: 4-speed
Speeds: 1.63, 3.13, 4.25,
   12.0 mph
Reverse: 2.50 mph
Shipping weight: 3,000 lbs.
Price, new: $1,600

Model 40T
Years built: 1953-1955
Built at: Dubuque, Iowa
Number built: 17,906
Configuration: Dual tricycle,
Single Front Wheel, or Wide-
front row crop

Wheels/Tires:
   Front: 5.00 x 15/6.00 x 16
   Rear: Single Front, 7.50 - 10
   9 or 10 - 34

Transmission: 4-speed
Speeds: 1.63, 3.13, 4.25,
   12.0 mph
Reverse: 2.50 mph
Shipping weight: 3,000 lbs.

Model 40V
Years built: 1955
Built at: Dubuque, Iowa
Number built: 329
Configuration: "Special" High-
   clearance standard tread

Wheels/Tires:
   Front: 5.00 x 15/6.00 x 16
   Rear: 9 or 10 - 34

Transmission: 4-speed
Speeds: 1.63, 3.13, 4.25,
   12.0 mph
Reverse: 2.50 mph
Shipping weight: 3,050 lbs.

Model 40H
Years built: 1955
Built at: Dubuque, Iowa
Number built: 294
Configuration: High-crop

Wheels/Tires:
   Front: 6.50 or 7.50 x 16
   Rear: 10 - 38 or 11 - 38

Transmission: 4-speed
Speeds: 1.63, 3.13, 4.25,
   12.0 mph
Reverse: 2.50 mph
Shipping weight: 3,400 lbs.

Crawler

Years built: 1953-1955
Built at: Dubuque, Iowa and Yakima, Washington
Number built: 11,689
Configuration: Crawler, three roller undercarriage to S/N 62263, four roller only to S/N 62363, four or five rollers optional thereafter

Track options: 10, 12, or 14 inch track shoes on 36, or 46 inch track centers

Transmission: 4-speed
Speeds: 0.82, 2.21, 2.95, 5.31 mph
Reverse: 1.60 mph
Shipping weight: 4,076 to 4,756 lbs., depending on track configuration
Price, new: $2,366 to $2,589, depending on track configuration

Engine options:
Bore & stroke: 4.00 x 4.00 inches, two cylinders
Displacement: 100.54 cid
Rated RPM: 1850
Fuel: gasoline or distillate
Compression ratio: (gasoline) 6.5:1
Ignition: coil
Cooling: thermosyphon

Serial numbers vs. year model

Beginning Serial Number	Year
Model 40S	
60001	1953
65927	1954
68881 (Last 71814)	1955
Model 40C	
60001	1953
62264	1954
66020 (Last 71689)	1955
Model 40T	
60001	1953
69475	1954
75179 (Last 77906)	1955
Model 40U	
60001	1954
62734 (Last 65208)	1955
Model 40V	
60001 (Last 60329)	1955
Model 40H	
60001 (Last 60294)	1955
Model 40W	
60001 (Last 61758)	1955

Nebraska Test Data

Model 40T
Test Number 503
Date: 9-1953
Max. belt. hp.: 23.51
Max. drawbar pull (lbs.): 3,022
Specific fuel consumption hp.-hrs./gal.: 11.16
Weight as tested (lbs.): 4,569

Model 40S
Test Number 504
Date: 9-1953
Max. belt. hp.: 23.21
Max. drawbar pull (lbs.): 2,543
Specific fuel consumption hp.-hrs./gal.: 11.27
Weight as tested (lbs.): 4,201

Model 40C
Test Number 505
Date: 9-1953
Max. belt. hp.: 23.64
Max. drawbar pull (lbs.): 4,515
Specific fuel consumption hp.-hrs./gal.: 11.61
Weight as tested (lbs.): 4,669

Model 40S (Distillate fuel)
Test Number 546
Date: 6-1955
Max. belt. hp.: 19.13
Max. drawbar pull (lbs.): 2,511
Specific fuel consumption hp.-hrs./gal.: 10.51
Weight as tested (lbs.): 4,169

John Deere Model 420

The Model 420 series of Dubuque tractors came out a year before the three-numbered tractors from Waterloo. The whole series was ready, and competition was tough, so the new CEO William Hewitt gave the go-ahead.

The first 420s had all-green bodies, rather than the two-tone paint scheme that followed in the 1957 model year. Interestingly, all 420s used the same serial numbering system, unlike that of the previous 40 Series.

Since the 420 was now competing in the $2,000 price category, it needed a bit more horsepower. It was a simple matter for Deere engineers to increase the bore of the Model 40 engine by 0.25 inches, upping the displacement to 113.3 cid. The compression ratio was also raised (on the gasoline engines) to 7.0:1. These changes gave about 20 percent more power.

All-fuel, or distillate, versions of the 420 were offered along with the gasoline types, although they were not a significant proportion of the total with only about 1,000 being sold. The all-fuel engine had a compression ratio of 5.5:1, close to that of older gasoline engines, but still offering a serious reduction in power and fuel economy when compared to the higher-compression gasoline engine.

In 1958, a LPG (Liquefied Petroleum Gas) option was offered. This engine used an 8.5:1 compression ratio to compensate for the lower BTU rating of LPG. This version was not tested at the University of Nebraska.

The Model 420 was introduced in 1956. It had important improvements over the 40 it replaced, such as a 20 percent power increase due in part to increased displacement.
Owner: Pollock Collection

The Model 420 also now had a pressurized radiator and a water pump. It was made in eight configurations with the 420V (Special) among the most rare.
Owner: Pollock Collection

To provide adequate cooling capacity for the more powerful engines, the thermocycle, or gravity-type cooling system of the Model 40 was replaced by a water pump system, with a pressurized radiator and a thermostat.

The same seven configurations of the Model 420 were offered as were available in the Model 40 tractors (plus industrial versions)as follows:
• S- Standard
• T- Row Crop, dual tricycle, wide front and single front wheel
• U- Utility
• V- Special Utility
• C - Crawler, both 4 and 5 roller undercarriages
• H – High Crop
• W – Row Crop-Utility

Other improvements included:
A cable driven tach/hour meter (replacing the electric type of the Model 40).

Power adjustable rear wheels for all models except for the H and V types.
• An improved final drive for the Model 420W.
• A 5-speed transmission option.
• A special 5-speed transmission option for use with trenchers for C and W tractors.
• A special 4-speed transmission option especially suited for loader tractors.
• A three-point hitch for the crawlers.
• An improved direction reverser.
• A live PTO option.
• Factory power steering.

For the 1958 model year the vertical steering wheel was replaced by one mounted on an angle. This proved to be a much more comfortable position and more like that offered by the competition. This feature wasn't available on the high crop or LPG tractors. Tractors without power steering got a larger diameter steering wheel.

Model 420
Data and Specifications

Overall Years Built: 1956-1958

Model 420S
Years built: 1956-1958
Built at: Dubuque, Iowa
Number built: 3,908
Configuration: Standard Tread

Wheels/Tires:
Front: 5.00 x 15/6.00 x 16
Rear: 9, 10 or 11 - 24

Shipping weight: 2,750 lbs.
Price, new: $1,976

Model 420U
Years built: 1956-1958
Built at: Dubuque, Iowa
Number built: 4,932
Configuration: Utility

Wheels/Tires:
Front: 5.00 x 15/6.00 x 16
Rear: 10 - 24 or 11-24
11 - 26 to 13-26

Shipping weight: 2,850 lbs.
Price, new: $2,170

Model 420W
Years built: 1956-1958
Built at: Dubuque, Iowa
Number built: 11,197
Configuration: Wide 2-row
Utility

Wheels/Tires:
Front: 5.00 x 15/6.00 x 16
Rear: 9 - 34 or 10 - 34

Shipping weight: 3,000 lbs.

Model 420T

Years built: 1956-1958
Built at: Dubuque, Iowa
Number built: 7,580
Configuration: Dual tricycle,
Single Front Wheel, or
Wide-front row crop

Wheels/Tires:
Front: 5.00 x 15/6.00 x 16
Rear: Single Front, 7.50 - 10
9 or 10 - 34

Shipping weight: 3,000 lbs.
Price, new: $2,090

Model 420V

Years built: 1956-1958
Built at: Dubuque, Iowa
Number built: 86
Configuration: "Special" High-
clearance standard tread

Wheels/Tires:
Front: 5.00 x 15/6.00 x 16
Rear: 9 or 10 - 34

Shipping weight: 3,050 lbs.
Price, new: $2,195

Model 420H

Years built: 1956-1958
Built at: Dubuque, Iowa
Number built: 610
Configuration: High-crop

Wheels/Tires:
Front: 6.50 or 7.50 x 16
Rear: 10 - 38 or 11 - 38

Shipping weight: 3,400 lbs.
Price, new: $2,328

Transmission, 4-Speed:
1st...............1.63 mph
2nd.............3.13 mph
3rd..............2.24 mph
4th..............12.0 mph
Reverse ......2.50 mph

Transmission, 5-Speed
(optional)
1st...............1.63 mph
2nd.............3.13 mph
3rd..............4.25 mph
4th..............6.25 mph
5th..............12.0 mph

Transmission, Special 4-speed
(for 420S)
1st...............2.00 mph
2nd.............3.75 mph
3rd..............5.00 mph
4th..............13.8 mph

420C Crawler

Years built: 1956-1958
Built at: Dubuque, Iowa and Yakima, Washington
Number built: 17,882
Configuration: Four or five rollers optional
Track options: 10, 12, or 14 inch track shoes on 36, or 46 inch track centers.
Transmission: 4-speed
Speeds, forward: 0.88, 2.25, 3.00, 5.25 mph
reverse: 1.75 mph
    5-speed forward: 0.88, 2.25, 3.00, 3.83, 5.25 mph
Shipping weight: 4,076 to 4,756 lbs, depending on track configuration.
Price, new: $2,316 to $2,599, depending on track configuration

Engine options:
Bore & Stroke: 4.25 x 4.00 inches, two cylinders
Displacement: 113.3 cid
Rated RPM: 1850
Fuel: gasoline, LPG or distillate
Compression Ratio: (gasoline) 7.0:1
                              (LPG) 8.5:1
                              (distillate) 5.15:1
Ignition: coil
Cooling: water pump

Beginning Serial Number	Year
80001	1956
107813	1957
127872	1958

Serial numbers vs. type

Type	80001-94818 Green		100001-119764 Green and Yellow		125002-136868 Slant Steer/1958	
	First	Last	First	Last	First	Last
T	80001	94750	100022	119764	125003	136864
S	80032	94727	100029	119710	125025	136866
C	80002	94815	100008	119761	125007	136795
W	80179	94818	100001	119763	125002	136868
V	80091	94363	100330	119064	125309	135242
H*	80231	94799	100515	119789	125132	136856
U**	80027	94794	100027	119709	125004	136867

*S/N 100515 and 100579 scrapped

** Does not include Holt forklift chassis

Nebraska Test Data
Model 420W
Test Number 599
Date: 10-1956
Max. belt. hp.: 27.25
Max. drawbar pull (lbs.): 3,790
Specific fuel consumption hp.-hrs./gal.: 11.72
Weight as tested (lbs.): 5,781

Model 420S Distillate fuel
Test Number 600
Date: 10-1956
Max. belt. hp.: 22.73
Max. drawbar pull (lbs.): 2,734
Specific fuel consumption hp.-hrs./gal.: 9.98
Weight as tested (lbs.): 4,311

Model 420C
Test Number 601
Date: 10-1956
Max. belt. hp.: 27.39
Max. drawbar pull (lbs.): 4,862
Specific fuel consumption hp.-hrs./gal.: 11.9
Weight as tested (lbs.): 5,079

The culmination of 44 years of two-cylinder tractor experience was the John Deere 430. Along with the rest of the 30 Series tractors, it was the epitome of a long and successful line. Following only two model years of production, the last of the two-cylinder tractors, and the tractor that had made John Deere famous, was being replaced by a completely revised "New Generation" of machines with 3, 4 and 6 cylinder engines.

Originally, when the New Generation tractor planning was undertaken in 1953, the model year for introduction was scheduled to be 1958. However, by early 1957, despite diverse applied resources, the entire line wasn't going to be ready.

Rather than lose the marketing shock-value by introducing the new line piecemeal, it was decided to freshen up the 20 series tractors and extend their lives two more years.

Model for model, therefore, the 430s, and last versions of the 420s are virtually identical. Therefore, performance was the same and testing at the University of Nebraska was not required. Introduced in August 1958, the main focus for the 430 was on comfort, convenience, safety and easier servicing. The same seven model types were offered as on the 420.

A few "F" versions were built (chassis only) for conversion by Holt to forklifts. No I (Industrial version) was offered, since the new Industrial Model 440 was also available in the 1958 to 1960 time period. The Model 440 was much the same as the 430 under the skin, but was heavier, more rugged and more expensive. It was available as a crawler and even with a 2-cylinder GM diesel.

All 440 versions were available with a three-point hitch with load and depth control and so did see some agricultural uses. All-yellow paint was an option for 430 tractors, and some, especially the S and U types, were used for industrial and highway applications.

Differences between the last of the 420s and the 430s included new "over-the-top" rear fenders for the T and W versions, the new "Float Ride" seat (an "armchair seat" was used on the C models), a new slanted dash with full instrumentation and finally, after S/N 155001, an optional 1000rpm PTO.* When the 440 model was introduced in 1958, it used a different engine block. This block had an oil dipstick plus filler/ breather on its right front. The last of the 420s used this engine, and so did the 430s.

*Not available for the crawler.

The 430 W was the row-crop-utility version; one of the seven configurations available. These included the Type S (Standard), Type U (Utility), Type W (Row-crop utility), Type H (Hi-Crop), Type V (Special), Type T (Row crop), and Type C (Crawler). Owner: Don Wolf, Ft. Wayne, Indiana

Featured on the Model 430 was a slanted dash panel with full instrumentation, an air cleaner system that took air in from an air pre-cleaner through an oil bath cleaner.
Owner: Jenna Ver Ploeg

The Model 430T is equipped with a Custom Powr-Trol three-point hitch. Duane Ver Ploeg, Sully, Iowa, did the restoration.
Owner: Kelsi Ver Ploeg

Model 430
Data and Specifications

Overall Years Built: 1959-1960

Model 430S
Years built: 1959-1960
Built at: Dubuque, Iowa
Number built: 1,809
Configuration: Standard Tread

Wheels/Tires:
　Front: 5.00 x 15/6.00 x 16
　Rear: 9, 10 or 11 - 24

Shipping weight: 2,750 lbs.

Model 430U
Years built: 1959-1960
Built at: Dubuque, Iowa
Number built: 1,353
Configuration: Utility

Wheels/Tires:
　Front: 5.00 x 15/6.00 x 16
　Rear: 10 - 24 or 11-24
　　　11 - 26 to 13-26

Shipping weight: 2,850 lbs.

Model 430W
Years built: 1959-1960
Built at: Dubuque, Iowa
Number built: 5,981
Configuration: Wide 2-row
　　Utility

Wheels/Tires:
　Front: 5.00 x 15/6.00 x 16
　Rear: 9 - 34 or 10 - 34

Shipping weight: 3,000 lbs.

Model 430T
Years built: 1959-1960
Built at: Dubuque, Iowa
Number built: 3,255
Configuration: Dual tricycle,
　Single Front Wheel, or
　Wide-front row crop

Wheels/Tires:
　Front: 5.00 x 15/6.00 x 16
　Rear: Single Front, 7.50 - 10
　　9 or 10 - 34

Shipping weight: 3,000 lbs.

Model 430V
Years built: 1959-1960
Built at: Dubuque, Iowa
Number built: 63
Configuration: "Special" High-
　clearance standard tread

Wheels/Tires:
　Front: 5.00 x 15/6.00 x 16
　Rear: 9 or 10 - 34

Shipping weight: 3,050 lbs.

Model 430H
Years built: 1959-1960
Built at: Dubuque, Iowa
Number built: 215
Configuration: High-crop

Wheels/Tires:
　Front: 6.50 or 7.50 x 16
　Rear: 10 - 38 or 11 - 38

Shipping weight: 3,400 lbs.

Transmission, 4-Speed:
1st.............1.63 mph
2nd............3.13 mph
3rd.............2.24 mph
4th.............12.0 mph
Reverse......2.50 mph

Transmission, 5-Speed
　(optional)
1st.............1.63 mph
2nd............3.13 mph
3rd.............4.25 mph
4th.............6.25 mph
5th.............12.0 mph

Transmission, Special 4-speed
　(for 430S)
1st...............2.00 mph
2nd.............3.75 mph
3rd..............5.00 mph
4th.............13.8 mph

430C Crawler

Years built: 1959-1960

Built at: Dubuque, Iowa and Yakima, Washington

Number built: 2,240

Configuration: Four or five rollers optional

Track options: 10, 12, or 14 inch track shoes on 36, or 46-inch track centers.

Transmission: 4-speed

Speeds, forward: 0.88, 2.25, 3.00, 5.25 mph

reverse: 1.75 mph

5-speed forward: 0.88, 2.25, 3.00, 3.83, 5.25 mph

Shipping weight: 4,156 to 4,775 lbs, depending on track configuration.

Price, new: $2,316 to $2,599, depending on track configuration

Engine options:

Bore & Stroke: 4.25 x 4.00 inches, two cylinders

Displacement: 113.3 cid

Rated RPM: 1850

Fuel: gasoline, LPG or distillate

Compression Ratio: (gasoline) 7.0:1

(LPG) 8.5:1

(distillate) 5.15:1

Ignition: coil

Cooling: water pump

Beginning Serial Number	Year
140001	1959
157024	1960

Serial Numbers vs Type

Type	First	Last
T	140006	161096
S	140027	160994
C	140001	161072
W	140003	16069
V	140557	161016
H	140071	161048
U	140010	161075

The Model 430T was the row-crop version of the popular 430. Owner: Kelsi Ver Ploeg

The Model 430U used the 113-cid overhead valve two-cylinder engine with a four-speed gearbox. A five-speed unit was optional, as was a direction reverser. Owner: Jenna Ver Ploeg

Model 435 Diesel

Diesel engines had become hot commodities early in the 1950s. Even though the price of gasoline was still relatively low, a big gas tractor such as a John Deere 70, could go through 35 gallons on a long summer day. An all-fuel 70 would consume even more! By comparison, a Diesel 70 would use only 20 gallons doing the same work. At that time, diesel fuel was cheaper than gasoline.

By the end of the decade, the push for diesels had migrated down to the smaller tractors, even though it was much harder to justify their extra cost in fuel savings.

Ford, British Fordson, Massey Ferguson and Oliver all had diesel utility tractors vying for the small tractor market. Deere, of course, was working on a whole new line of multi-cylinder diesel engines (as well as gasoline and all-fuel) for the "New Generation" line of tractors to be unveiled in August of 1960.

A new 30-hp diesel engine was needed partly as a competitive stopgap measure, partly to allay fears by dealers and customers that Deere was abandoning the market segment, and partly to provide additional cover for the highly secret New Generation activity.

At first, Deere engineers tried to make a diesel out of the 113-cid 2-cylinder engine. It was soon determined that excessive modifications would be required that weren't economically justified. Early in 1958, the Industrial Group at Deere had launched its Model 440 industrial tractor. The 440 was a beefed up agricultural Model 430. To expedite getting a diesel for the 440, a GM Diesel 2-53 engine was chosen.

General Motors had pioneered the modular 2-cycle diesels. They had already been on the market for a number of years. There were several sizes of piston displacement to choose from 53 cid per cylinder to over 100 cid per cylinder.

Since the engines were of the 2-cycle type, the customer could specify the number of cylinders wanted to get the horsepower needed. The 2-53 engine had 2 cylinders of 53 cubic inches of displacement each, or 106 cid total. As a 2-cycle engine, with two power strokes per revolution, its power output was more like

The 435 was similar to the Model 430, but had about 10 percent more horsepower. Gear ratios were adjusted to make use of the extra power in faster working speeds. The engine, obtained from General Motors, was their 2-53 two-cycle-type with blower-scavenged exhaust.
Owner: Don Wolf, Ft. Wayne, Indiana

This Model 435 decal is showing the effects of many years of exposure.

that of a four. Also inherent with the 2-cycle engine was its sound. It sounded like it was turning twice as fast as it really was.

The GM engine used only exhaust valves. Intake air arrived through a Rootes-type blower through ports in the sides of the cylinder wall. When the piston traveled down, the exhaust valve opened and the piston uncovered the ports. Pressurized air from the blower rushed in, purging the exhaust gasses out through the exhaust valve. As the piston started up, the ports were covered and the exhaust valve closed. Near the top of the stroke, fuel was injected.

Auto ignition of the fuel, due to the heat of compression, started the piston downward, and the cycle started over again. Although the blower provided some supercharging, its purpose was to expel the burnt gasses and introduce fresh air for the next cycle.

To reduce the number of peculiar parts, the 435 was offered only in the row crop utility style. That had proven to be the most popular of the styles offered for the 420/430. It also matched the configuration of the already beefed up Industrial 440. The GM engine was considerably heavier, and had significantly more power

and torque, so strengthening was done where needed.

To aid in handling the increased torque, gear ratios were changed so the 435 was faster in its working gears. Since horsepower (torque times speed) is the rate of doing work, this change kept drive train torque approximately the same as on the 430.

The list of options was quite extensive for the Model 435. Standard equipment included small tires, three-point hitch with Touch-O-Matic draft control and a 560 rpm PTO.

Options included:
- Rear wheel weights (Front weights were deemed unnecessary due to the weight of the engine.)
- Float-Ride seat.
- Power steering. (after S/N 436452)
- 1000 rpm PTO.
- Remote hydraulics.
- 5-speed transmission.
- Underneath exhaust.
- Hour meter (electric).
- Larger tires and wheels, with or without power adjust.
- Dual Touch-O-Matic (late in production).

Model 435 Diesel
Data and Specifications

The engine utilized exhaust valves only. Intake air entered through ports when the pistons were at the bottom of their stroke. Shown is a 1960 Model 435 owned by Don Wolf, Ft. Wayne, Indiana.
Owner: Don Wolf, Ft. Wayne, Indiana

Years Built: 1959
Built at: Dubuque, Iowa
Number built: 4,625
Configuration: Row Crop Utility

Wheels/Tires:
    Rear: 9-34, 10-34 or 12-28
    Front: 5.00-15 or 6.00-16

Transmission:

	5-Speed		4-Speed	
Speeds:	1	1.88 mph	1	1.88 mph
	2	3.50 mph	2	3.50 mph
	3	4.75 mph	3	4.75 mph
	4	7.00 mph	4	13.5 mph
	5	13.5 mph		
Reverse:		2.88 mph		2.88 mph

Electrical System: 12-Volt
Shipping Weight: 4,100lbs
Price, New: $3,190

Serial Numbers vs. Year Model

Serial Numbers	Year
435001-435960	4/1959-12/1959
435961-439626	1/1960-2/1960

Nebraska Test Data
Test Number 716
Date: 9-1959
Max. belt. hp.: 32.91
Max. drawbar hp.: 27.59
Specific fuel consumption hp.-hrs./gal.:
    14.35
Weight as tested (lbs.): 6,057

At the middle of the 20th century, tractors with more than 50 horsepower were rare. This was due, in large part, to their inordinate fuel consumption. Tractors such as the big Minneapolis-Moline, or Massey-Harris 55 were fitted with large fuel tanks to reduce mid-day refueling requirements.

As much as 75 gallons of fuel could be consumed in a hard day's work. Just having a week's worth of fuel on hand could be a problem for the farmer. Large-acreage farmers were converting to tractors with diesel engines, and that generally meant limited choices, or going to crawlers.

The diesel engine was invented by German engineer Dr. Rudolf Christian Karl Diesel. Born in Paris in 1858 of German parents, Rudolf studied engineering in England and Germany. In 1892, he obtained a patent for the engine that bears his name. The engine was based on the four-cycle principle developed by Nicolas Otto.

The difference was Diesel's engine used a compression ratio of 15:1, rather than 4 or 5:1 as was common at the time. Air heated by compression to that pressure (about 225 psi) was hot enough to ignite fuel oil injected into the combustion chamber. No throttle was needed as power was regulated by the amount of fuel injected. The quantity of air taken in by the engine was consistent with the engine's displacement.

This feature was one of the main reasons for the engine's frugality. It ran at a much leaner mixture and improved volumetric efficiency (due in part to the fact there was no choking effect from a carburetor).

Dr. Diesel's engine took many years of development before its use in wheel tractors was practical. The engine-driven variable fuel injector system was, perhaps, the main pacing item that prevented the use of the engine in other than stationary or marine applications. Metallurgy was another restriction.

The Model R was introduced in 1949 and produced through 1954. Sales people feared that it wouldn't be accepted, so the D, which it was intended to replace, was kept in production until early 1953.

Diesel's first engine weighed 9,000 lbs. and produced only 20 hp. German companies Junkers, Mercedes-Benz and Maybach, and the French company Peugeot, pioneered development of the engine. International Harvester became interested in diesel development as early as 1916, but World War I prevented flow of information, at least from Germany.

By the late 1920s, both I-H and Caterpillar were having success with diesel engine development. Caterpillar was first into diesel tractor production with its 1931 Diesel Sixty. Harvester was the first with a diesel wheel tractor in 1935 with its WD-40.

In 1935, Deere Chief Engineer Barrett Rich concluded that diesel power was here to stay and had Deere embark on a series of studies. Interestingly, Deere and Caterpillar concluded an agreement in that same year for joint dealerships (which essentially meant that Deere would stick to wheel tractors and Cat would do only crawlers).

There is no official record of collaboration on diesel engines, but it is notable that Deere's first diesel had the same bore and stroke as the Caterpillar RD-8, which was in development at the same time.

By 1940, Deere's two-cylinder diesel had been developed to the point where it was ready to go in a tractor. Eight experimental MX tractors were built for it. Testing of these eight continued to the end of 1941. The tractor was then completely redesigned to overcome all weaknesses found.

World War II slowed progress on the project considerably, but by 1944 the revised MX was ready for the field. Testing then lasted into 1947, followed by another complete redesign. This tractor was the Model R.

Speculation has it that after row crop tractors came along at Deere, standard tread machines such as the D, were referred to as "Regulars." Standard tread versions of the Models A and B were labeled AR and BR (for regular). The big diesel-plowing tractor, designed to replace the Model D, was called the R.

When the Model R was introduced in 1949, sales people feared it would not be accepted. The D was kept in production for four more years. Advertising pointed out similarities: two-cylinder engine, ruggedness and simplicity. Advantages were also pointed out including diesel economy, five-speed gearbox (rather than three), all-gear drive (the D's final drive was chain), and enough power to handle 5 or 6 plow bottoms (the D could handle 3 or 4). There was also the live PTO and hydraulics (for remote cylinders).

The R could plow a 40 in a 12-hour day on less than 25 gallons of diesel fuel. The D would take two days and about 70 gallons of fuel. Sales of the D plummeted.

The Model R is noteworthy from other standpoints as well. It had record-breaking fuel economy, besting even the record held by Caterpillar. It was the first Deere to offer live PTO and hydraulics and it was the first Deere wheel tractor to offer a factory cab.

Standard equipment included starter (pony), lights, battery (12V), belt pulley, hour meter, muffler and air cleaner. Options included the various wheels and tires shown below, live PTO, live hydraulics, radiator shutter, foam rubber seat cushion, heavy-load-reduced speed transmission and wheel weights.

It was the first Deere wheel tractor to offer a factory cab. Standard equipment included a gasoline 25-cid starting (pony) motor, lights, 12 volt battery, belt pulley, hour meter, muffler and air cleaner.

Model R
Data and Specifications

Overall Years Built: 1949-1954
Built At: Waterloo, Iowa
Available configurations: Standard tread –
(Wheatland or rice)

Wheels/Tires:
Front: 7.50-18 standard
Rear: 14-34 standard, 15-34 optional, 18-26 standard for rice duty.

Steel Wheels:
Front: 30 x 6 inches
Rear: 54 x 12 inches

Engine: Side-by-side horizontal diesel, overhead valve, four-cycle
Number of Cylinders: 2
Bore & stroke: 5.75 x 8.00 inches
Displacement: 416 cid
Rated RPM: 1,000
Compression Ratio: 16:1
Cooling: Thermosyphon
Clutch: 9.25 in diameter, 6-disks, hand-lever operated
Starter: Pony motor, 2-cylinder horizontally opposed, four-cycle.
Displacement: 25 cid. Approximately 10 hp @ 4,000 rpm.
Electric start and magneto ignition.

Transmission:
(Standard)

Gear	Speed
1	2.125 mph
2	3.333 mph
3	4.250 mph
4	5.333 mph
5	11.50 mph*
Reverse	2.50 mph

*5th gear blocked when furnished with steel wheels

(Optional)

1	2.25 mph
2	3.50 mph
3	4.00 mph
4	4.50 mph
5	5.50 mph
Reverse	2.50 mph

Shipping Weight: 7,182 lbs. standard equipment
7,081 lbs. on steel
7,652 lbs. full rice equipment

Price, New: $3,650 Standard equipment, 1954
$3,319 Standard equipment on steel
$4,240 Full rice equipped

Nebraska Test Data
Test Number 406
Date: 4-1949
Max. belt. hp.: 50.96
Max. available drawbar pull lbs.: 6,644
Specific fuel consumption hp.-hrs./gal.: 17.35
Weight as tested (lbs.): 9,773

Serial Numbers vs. Year Model

Year	Beginning Serial Number
1949	1000
1950	2415
1951	6368
1952	9293
1953	15093
1954	19093

Production Totals
Shipped to US and Canada: 17,563
Exported to other countries: 3,570
Serial numbers not used, or scrapped: 160

Model 80

The John Deere two-number tractors entered the market place piecemeal. The 50 and 60 came out in 1952, the 40 and 70 in 1953, but the new 80 did not make the scene until 1955. That gave the Model R a six-year production run, but the 80 only got a little over a year before being replaced by the 820. That was the shortest run of any Deere tractor.

Best guess as to the reason for this is the Model R was holding its own with the competition, and the Deere engineers had their hands full with the Model 70 diesel and other new tractors.

The diesel engine for the Model 70 row crop tractor was a new design with improvements over that of the R. As this engine was being developed in 1950 and '51, it was decided that the Model 80 engine would incorporate these improvements as well.

The influential Minneapolis Sales Branch was calling for more power from the top-of-the-line plowing tractor. Their customers wanted 75 horsepower, instead of the 50+ horsepower the R was delivering. By taking the 6.125-inch bore and combustion chambers of the new 70 engine while retaining the 8-inch stroke of the

R, displacement would be up from 416 cid to 471.5 cid. That, plus an increase in the speed from 1000 rpm to 1125 rpm, would give the new 80 two-thirds more power.

It was still short of the desire of the Minneapolis Sales Branch (68 hp rather than 75 hp), but was a substantial improvement. To handle the higher rpm, the new 80 engine was given a center bearing on the crankshaft similar to that developed for the Model 70 engine.

Also from the Model 70 was a new, more powerful, Vee-4 starter (pony) engine. This "pony motor" took up less space than the old two-cylinder-opposed starting engine of the Model R, and this was important in order to fit it under the slimmer hood of the row crop 70. The smaller starter made it possible to eliminate bevel gears on both the 70 and the 80.

The additional horsepower output of the new diesel that powered the 80 required the use of a water pump cooling system. A copper shortage in that time period also caused more steel to be used for radiators. With the use of steel came pressurized systems in order to obtain

Six years after its introduction, in 1955, the Model R was replaced by the Model 80. The popularity of Deere's first diesel accounts for the delay. The 80 looks much like the R, except for the flywheel cover. It was teardrop-shaped on the 80 and round on the R.

the same heat exchange rate as with copper radiators and the thermosyphon system. The 80 had a pressurized radiator, pressure cap and a water pump.

The optional "Powr-Trol" hydraulic system enabled the operator to control two remote cylinders. The system provided 1,000 psi and 13 gpm. A major improvement on the 80 was the use of a hydraulic pump that was driven directly by the engine. On the Model R, the pump was driven by the PTO, and some failures were experienced because of this parasitic load on the PTO drive.

Customer deliveries of the Model 80 began in August of 1955, even though the design was ready for production in February. This leisurely pace allowed the sale of a backlog of Model R tractors on dealer lots.

Steel wheels were still an option, since there were conditions in the rice fields wherein steel wheels, with their gripping lugs, excelled. A steel "tire" was developed that fit onto the rear wheel. This made switching from steel to rubber and back again easier.

Almost all 80s were delivered with the optional power steering.

Other options included:
- Factory cab
- Weather break
- Fender extensions
- Cigar lighter
- Rubber seat cushion

Standard features of the Model 80 were:
- Speed-hour meter
- Electric fuel gauge
- Fenders
- Muffler
- Swinging drawbar
- Adjustable spring seat
- Belt pulley
- Oil and air filters
- Battery and lights

The last Model 80 rolled off the assembly line in July, 1956.

An increase in displacement gave the Model R almost one-third more horsepower. The 80 shown is a 1955 model.

Model 80
Data and Specifications

Overall Years Built: 1955-1956

Built at: Waterloo, Iowa

Available configurations: Standard tread –
    (Wheatland, or rice)

Wheels/Tires:
    Front: 7.50-18 standard (single rib for rice
        duty)
    Rear: 14-34 standard, 15-34 optional, 18-26
    standard for rice duty
Steel Wheels
    Front: 30 x 6 inches
    Rear: 54 x 12 inches

Engine: Side-by-side Horizontal Diesel, Overhead
    Valve, Four-cycle
Number of Cylinders: 2
Bore & Stroke: 6.125 x 8.00 inches
    Displacement: 471.5 cid
Rated RPM: 1,125
Compression Ratio: 16:1
Cooling: Thermostat and pump
Clutch: 9.25 in. diaphragm, 8-disks, hand-lever
    operated
Starter: Pony Motor, 4-cylinder Vee-type, four-
    cycle.
Displacement: 18.8 cid. Approximately 12 hp @
    5,500 rpm.
Electric start, 6v with magneto ignition.

Transmission: (Standard)

Gear	Speed
1	2.50 mph*
2	3.50 mph
3	4.50 mph
4	5.333 mph
5	6.75 mph
6	12.25 mph
Reverse	2.66 mph

*Optional slow-speed first gear   1.75 mph

Shipping Weight: 7,555 lbs. Standard equipment
                7,900 lbs. Full rice equipment

Price, New: $4,205 Standard equipment, 1956
            $4,465 Full rice equipment

Nebraska Test Data
Test Number 567
Date: 10-1955
Max. belt. hp.: 67.6
Max. available drawbar pull lbs.: 7,394
Specific fuel consumption hp.-hrs./gal.: 17.58
Weight as tested (lbs.): 11,495

Serial Numbers vs. Year Model

Year	Beginning Serial Number
1955	8000001
1956	8000775
Last Serial Number	8003500

Production Totals
Shipped to US and Canada: 3,286
Exported to other countries: 199
Serial numbers not used, or scrapped: 15

The first prototype John Deere Model 820 tractor was most likely made from a production Model 80. That is an indication of how minor the change was between the two. The only external differences were in the yellow paint stripe on the hood and the elephant ear fenders (they were introduced before on the Models 60 and 70 standards).

There were a few internal improvements, however. There were new 10-inch brakes, increased from 9 inches on the 80. There was a new power steering system, improvements to the final drive, there was the new optional "Float Ride" seat, and there was a new steel cab with improved sealing and soundproofing. Although originally, the engine had the same power as the 80, the connecting rods were beefed up and there were minor improvements in cooling and lubrication systems.

Full rice field equipment now came as a package called "Rice Special." Besides a decal declaring that a tractor was a "Rice Special" the buyer got either 15-34 or 23.1-26 rear tires with Cane and Rice treads. Front tires sported a single rib. The rear axle and brakes were protected from the mud by special shields. Steel "tires" were also available upon special request.

For the 1958 model year, engine improvements put the power of the 820 over the 75 horsepower mark (75.6 hp corrected to sea level, standard day conditions). The improvements were in the form of new fuel injectors and revised heads and combustion chambers. There were other minor improvements made at the same time, improvements that made starting easier and made the tractor more reliable. Also changed at that time (Serial Number 8203100) was the color of the instrument panel from green to black. Hence 820 (Improved) tractors are known as "Black Dash" tractors.

Besides the Float Ride seat and cab, options included a new oval muffler, a foot operated power control (gas pedal), a cigar lighter, an air intake pre-cleaner, Custom Powr-Trol hydraulics, and a creeper first gear.

The 820 was available with Custom Powr-Trol, the dual, live hydraulic system that could control two separate remote hydraulic cylinders. Power steering was standard on the 820.

Overall Years Built: 1957-1958

Built at: Waterloo, Iowa

Available configurations: Standard tread –
   (Wheatland, or rice)

Note: Serial Number 8200000 (1957) to Serial
   Number 8207078 (1958) are known as "Green-
   Dash" tractors. These have the same engine
   power as the Model 80. Serial Number 8203100
   (1958) and on, are known as "Black-Dash"
   tractors. Engine improvements gave 12 percent
   more power.

Wheels/Tires:
   Front: 7.50-18 standard (single rib for rice
      duty)
   Rear: 14-34 standard, 15-34 optional, 18-26
      standard for rice duty, 23.1-26 optional.
Steel Wheels:
   Front: 30 x 6 inches
   Rear: 54 x 12 inches
             (bolt-on steel "tires" available)

Engine: Side-by-side Horizontal Diesel, Overhead
   Valve, Four-cycle
Number of Cylinders: 2
Bore & Stroke: 6.125 x 8.00 inches
   Displacement: 471.5 cid
Rated RPM: 1,125
Compression Ratio: 16:1
Cooling: Thermostat and pump
Clutch: 9.25 in. diaphragm, 8-disks, hand-lever
   operated
Starter: Pony Motor, 4-cylinder Vee-type, four-
   cycle.
Displacement: 18.8 cid. Approximately 12 hp @
   5,500 rpm.
Electric start, 6v with magneto ignition.

Transmission: (Standard)

Gear	Speed
1	2.33 mph*
2	3.50 mph
3	4.50 mph
4	5.333 mph
5	6.75 mph
6	12.25 mph
Reverse	2.66 mph

*Optional slow-speed first gear   1.75 mph

Shipping Weight: 7,855 lbs. Standard equipment
   7,900 lbs. Full rice equipment

Price, New: $4,850 Standard equipment, 1957
   $5,287 Full rice equipment

Nebraska Test Data
Test Number 632
Date: 10-1957*
Max. belt. hp.: 72.82
Max. available drawbar pull lbs.: 8,667
Specific fuel consumption hp.-hrs./gal.: 17.28
Weight as tested (lbs.): 11,995
* Black Dash Model 820

Model 820 Serial Number vs. Year Model

Year	First and Last Serial Numbers
1957	8200000-8203036 (Green Dash)
1958	8203100-8207080 (Black Dash)

Production Totals
   Shipped to U.S. and Canada: 5,950
   Exported to other countries: 909
   Serial numbers not used, or scrapped: 159
   Total 820 tractors built: 7,018

Comparisons

Make/model	No. of cylinders.	Displacement, cid	PTO hp	Drawbar pull, lbs.	Test weight, lbs.
IH 660D	6	281	78.78	N/A**	15,255
Oliver 990GM	3	213*	84.10	12,629	16,665

*2-cycle General Motors 3-71 diesel with blower.

**Test procedures changed to include maximum drawbar horsepower of 64.43.

The John Deere Model 830 was the top of the line and the last of the line of two-cylinder tractors. They were big, heavy and impressive. Advertising copy of the era called the 830 "Mr. Mighty," and truly it was.

The 830 had the same power as the 820, the tractor it replaced in 1959, and was not tested at the University of Nebraska. The Dreyfuss industrial design team was given a free hand to work other cosmetic and ergonomic improvements. International Harvester had unveiled a new Model 660 and Case the 900B in 1959. All were in the same power class, so the advent of the newly styled John Deere 830 helped the dealers compete.

Besides the new, rounded sheet metal, the 830 had a new quieting oval muffler, improved controls and instruments, optional power steering and Float-Ride seat. A major change was the availability of a direct electric start option, using two 12-volt batteries in series. A 24-volt starting motor also was used in place of the V-4 Pony motor.

A Rice Special package, consisting of special mud protection for the brakes and axle and cane/rice tires, was available with a multitude of special wheels (including steel).

Other options included single, or dual hydraulics, a foot pedal accelerator, special creeper gear transmission, heating elements for oil and water to ease cold weather starting and a cigarette lighter. New for John Deere tractors with the 830 was an optional factory cab.

Since Model 80 and 820 tractors had been pressed into industrial and construction duties, and since there had been some structural failures, a heavy-duty version was offered. These were interspersed with the regular 830s in the serial number sequence. These had strengthened front and rear axles, and drawbars and a variety of tire options.

Finally, 130 of the Model 830 tractors were assembled in Deere's Monterrey, Mexico, plant. Four blocks of serial numbers were assigned to take care of orders as they came in.

These were as follows:

Block 1   8300800-8300829
Block 2   8301600-8301616
Block 3   8303700-8303727
Block 4   8304900-8304943

Most of these tractors were believed to have electric start, single hydraulics and no other options.

The 830 was the ultimate "Wheatland", or plowing tractor. It was only made as a standard-tread, and only with a diesel engine.
Owner: Robert Couch, Kramer, North Dakota

The engine had a displacement of 471.5 cubic inches. It produced 75.6 belt horsepower at 1,125rpm. Owner: Robert Couch, Kramer, North Dakota

Model 830
Data and Specifications

Overall Years Built: 1958-1960
Built at: Waterloo, Iowa

Available configurations: Standard tread –
    (wheatland, or rice)

Wheels/Tires:
    Front: 7.50-18 standard (single rib for rice duty)
    Rear: 14-34, 15-34, 18-26 standard for duty
        15-34 or 18-26 cane and rice duty

Steel Wheels
    Front: 30 x 6 inches
    Rear: 54 x 12 inches (bolt-on steel "tires"
    available)

Engine: Side-by-side horizontal diesel, overhead
    valve, four-cycle
Number of Cylinders: 2
Bore & Stroke: 6.125 x 8.00 inches
Displacement: 471.5 cid
Rated RPM: 1,125
Compression Ratio: 16:1
Cooling: Thermostat and pump
Clutch: 9.25 in. diameter, 8-disks, hand lever
    operated
Starter: Pony Motor, 4-cylinder Vee-type, four-
    cycle.
Displacement: 18.8 cid. Approximately 12 hp @
    5,500rpm.
Electric start, 6v with magneto ignition.
Direct electric start, 24-volt

Transmission: (Standard)

Gear	Speed
1	2.33 mph*
2	3.50 mph
3	4.50 mph
4	5.333 mph
5	6.75 mph
6	12.25 mph
Reverse	2.66 mph

*Optional slow-speed first gear 1.75 mph

Shipping weight: 7,855 lbs. Standard equipment*
              7,900 lbs. Full rice equipment*
*Add approximately 1,000 lbs for optional power
    steering, PTO and hydraulics.

Price, new: $5,317 Standard equipment, 1960
           $5,796 Full rice equipment

Nebraska Test Data
Not tested – same as 820

Model 830 serial number vs. year model

Year	First and Last Serial Numbers
1959	830000-8304192
1960	8304193-8306891

Total number of 830 production (including
    industrial) 6,715
830 tractors assembled in Mexico: 130
Serial numbers not used, or scrapped: 46
830 tractors exported: 494

The final version of the venerable Model B came out in 1947. Deere & Co. was not content to leave well enough alone, however, and by 1949 was working on an improved model. This time, increased power was not deemed necessary, just improvements in operator convenience, comfort and driveability. Styling would be upgraded to match the new Model R.

Two main improvements were live hydraulics and PTO. The Canadian Cockshutt company had been the first to offer a live PTO on their 1946 Model 30. This feature was incorporated into the Model 50 as an option (either a live PTO, or none). It was a remarkable improvement, which allowed the tractor to be declutched and stopped while the PTO continued to run the machinery being powered, such as a baler or a combine. Deere had offered a live hydraulic option for the latest Model B tractors, so this feature was simply made standard on the 50.

By 1951, a decision was made to change the entire line of model designators from letters to numbers. Deere wanted a clear line of demarcation between what it saw as "pre-war" and "post-war" tractors. The newly styled line with new model numbers would provide that marketing feature.

It was at this time that a decision was also made to drop the stylish, but troublesome, pressed steel frame.

Since the Models M and 40 had replaced the standard tread and orchard versions of the Model B, the new Model 50 was made only as a row-crop tractor. In fact, the wide (W), high (H) and narrow (N) designators were also dropped, even though those variations of the basic 50 were still available.

The 50 was much like the late Model Bs, except it had reverted to the cast angle-iron frame instead of the Bs pressed steel type. It also had a larger fuel tank and an increased capacity hydraulic system.
Owner: Marv Mathiowetz, Princeton, Minnesota.

The Model 50 replaced the Model B in 1952.
Owner: Marv Mathiowetz, Princeton, Minnesota.

Initially, company records maintained the front-end suffix letters, but that was soon dropped (after S/N 5001101). A two-piece front-end support was used when the wide-front option was exercised. This two-piece "pedestal" (as it was called) allowed easy conversion between front-end types. At S/N 5014633, the single-piece pedestal was dropped and the two-piece version became standard.

A Roll-O-Matic front axle was virtually standard on tractors with dual narrow fronts, though non-Roll-O-Matic axles were listed as available. Steel front wheels with a non-Roll-O-Matic axle were carried as optional equipment.

One of the nicest new features on the Model 50 was the two-barrel carburetor. Because of the uneven firing of the Deere two-cylinder engine, the right cylinder tended to get a little less gas than the left (which got first chance at it).

Rather than having a single-throat carburetor feeding both cylinders, Deere and carburetor manufacturer Marvel-Schebler tried a dual-throat, or two-barrel unit. Along with modifications to the manifold and cylinder heads, this resulted in greatly improved performance and economy, and also made for easier starting. The Model 50 is hard to beat in smooth, slow idling as well.

Other features and options:

Rack and pinion rear wheel tread adjustment.

The old spline-type rear wheel adjustments worked well enough until lack of grease and rust made it difficult to get the wheels to slide on the axles. The mechanical advantage of the "geared" adjustment overcame that problem.

New rear wheels eliminated the need to switch wheels to the other side of the tractor to get maximum width.

Operator ease and comfort were provided by lengthening the clutch and throttle levers and by incorporating an adjustable seat back. A lighted instrument panel is featured along with a tachometer/hour meter. Power steering became an option at S/N 5020400.

An automatic (thermostat) controlled radiator

shutter was initially used. At S/N 5016615, an in-line thermostat was incorporated along with a pressurized steel radiator. This change was partly to save copper, which was at that time, a Korean War-critical material.

In January 1955, the LPG version of the Model 50 became available at S/N 5024000. Besides the increased compression ratio, these engines had hardened valve seats.

Finally, there were about 200 special Model 50 tractors sold to the Barber-Greene Company of Aurora, Illinois. These were incorporated into their Model 550 Loader. Barber-Greene was known for industrial trenchers and other such equipment. The Model 550 loader picked up heavy materials from windrows and deposited them in a pacing truck.

A live PTO was an option. The 190 cid two-cylinder engine was available configured for gasoline, LPG or "All-Fuel" (distillate or gasoline). Owner: Marv Mathiowetz, Princeton, Minnesota.

Model 50
Data and Specifications

Overall years built: 1952-1956 (Note: Since Model B production continued well into 1952, and Model 50 volume production did not start until October 1952, the more correct first model year for the Model 50 is 1953.)

Overall Serial Numbers: 5000001-5033751

Number built: 32,574

Built at: Waterloo, Iowa

Front and Rear Axle Options:

Dual tricycle front/ rack & pinion adjustable rear axle.

Adjustable wide front/ rack & pinion adjustable rear axle.

Single front wheel / rack & pinion adjustable rear axle.

Adjustable wide front, longer spindles/ longer rack & pinion adjustable rear axle.

Wheels/Tires

Front: 5.50-16 (dual, or wide front)
      9.00-10 (single front wheel)

Rear: 10/11-38
      9/11-42 (optional)

Length: 132.75 inches

Height (to top of hood): 59.9 inches

Weight: 4,435 lbs. (dual tricycle configuration)

Engine:

Type: Two-cylinder, four-stroke horizontal, side-by-side with pistons operating in opposition.

Bore & Stroke: 4.6875 x 5.50 inches

Displacement: 190.4 cid

Rated RPM: 1,250

Compression Ratio

Gasoline: 6.10:1

All-Fuel: 5.35:1

LPG: 8.00:1

Carburetor

Gasoline (S/N 5000001-5022299) Marvel-Schebler DLTX-75

 (S/N 5022300+) Marvel-Schebler DLTX-86

All-Fuel (S/N 5000001-5105950) Marvel-Schebler DLTX-73

 (S/N 5015951+) Marvel-Schebler DLTX-83

LPG (S/N 5024000-5030599) John Deere AB4872R

 (S/N 5030600+) John Deere AB4953R

Electrical: 12 Volt system with two 6-volt batteries under the seat.

A generator, rather than an alternator was used.

Distributor ignition with automatic spark advance.

Front and rear lights standard.

Transmission:

Gear speed	Speed (mph)
1	1.50
2	2.50
3	3.50
4	4.50
5	5.75
6	10.00
reverse	2.50

Price, New: $2,100

Year Model vs Beginning Serial Number

Year	Beginning Serial Number
1953	5000001
1954	5014620
1955	5020400
1956	5029200

Serial number notes:

Serial Numbers 5020355 to 5020399 and 5029060 to 5029199 were not assigned in order to start model years 1955 and 1956 with round numbers.

	First	Last	Total Built
Gasoline	5000001	5033751	29,746 (includes those built for Barber-Greene)
All-Fuel	5000171	5033741	2,097
LPG	5024000	5033729	731

Nebraska Test Data

Model 50 gasoline
Test Number 486
Date: 10-1952
Max. belt. hp.: 28.55
Max. drawbar pull lbs.: 3,504
Specific fuel consumption hp.-hrs./gal.: 11.82
Weight as tested (lbs.): 5,433

Model 50 distillate
Test Number 507
Date: 9-1953
Max. belt. hp.: 23.64
Max. drawbar pull lbs.: 3,583
Specific fuel consumption hp.-hrs./gal.: 11.09
Weight as tested (lbs.): 5,527

Model 50 LPG
Test Number 540
Date: 5-1955
Max. belt. hp.: 30.18
Max. drawbar pull lbs.: 3,466
Specific fuel consumption hp.-hrs./gal.: 9.13
Weight as tested (lbs.): 5,340

Engine improvements gave the 50 about 10 percent more power than the B. The dome-shaped objects on both sides of the engine are spark plug protective covers.
Owner: Marv Mathiowetz, Princeton, Minnesota.

This John Deere Model 50 carries an optional Killefer tool bar on an 801 three-point hitch.
Owner: Keller Collection

Model 520

Competition in the tractor business during the mid-1950s kept the engineers at Deere busy. International Harvester had introduced some especially nice tractors in 1955. Their Model 300, an outgrowth of the old Model H and the traditional counterpart to the Deere B, compared favorably to the Deere Model 60 in power and drawbar pull.

The I-H tractors had five-speed transmissions with the power-shift Torque Amplifier giving 10 speeds forward and two in reverse, while the Deere tractors had only six speeds. At the same time, the Deere Models 50 and 40 were overlapping in capability leading to some customer confusion. The Deere New Generation tractors were already in the works for introduction in 1960, but something would have to be done in the mean time.

Marketing deemed the tractor line generally needed about 20 percent more horsepower per model – hence,

the "Twenty Series" was conceived. The new 520 would be unveiled as a 1957 model replacing the Model 50.

Experimental work being done for the New Generation engines had yielded some marked improvements in combustion chamber design. These would be incorporated into a new engine for the 520. Though it would have the same bore and stroke as the Model 50 engine, the engine for the 520 would be completely new.

The new combustion chamber design required the relocation of the spark plugs from the block to the head. Improved combustion allowed for raising the compression ratio to 7:1 (up from 6.1:1) for the gasoline version. To improve spark timing the distributor was relocated to the main case where it was driven by the camshaft.

This eliminated the slack, or lash, in the distributor drive. Since the cam runs at half engine speed, the

Most of these were shipped to California for vegetable cultivation. The single front wheel version was ideal for running down narrow rows.
Owner: Keller Collection

"problem" of spark-on-the exhaust-stroke, common to previous Deere two-cylinder engines was eliminated (really only a problem for LPG tractors). The new engine would also feature aluminum pistons, a forged crankshaft and stronger connecting rods.

All these improvements allowed a higher rated speed of 1,325 rpm, up from 1,250 rpm for the Model 50. The horsepower rose by over 20 percent and fuel economy was also improved.

The 520 tractor was strengthened as necessary to handle the increased power. The frosting on the competitive cake was the new Custom Powr-Trol implement system. It featured a proper category 1 or 2 three-point hitch with both draft and position control. The new system had the hydraulic power, flexibility and control that competitive systems lacked and made the 520 into a really useful and productive tractor. The 520 could handle three 14-inch plow bottoms, or four-row planters and cultivators.

Operator comfort and convenience was also a major concern of the 520's designers. Power steering was available and a new Float-Ride seat, cushioned by rubber torsion springs that could be adjusted to the driver's weight, was also optional. The optional tachometer/hour meter was placed in the center of the dash panel, rather than on an add-on panel as it had been. The size of the fuel tank was increased from 15.5 to 18 gallons, and a panel fuel gauge was made an option.

Power adjustable rear wheels became an option in 1958. A new black dash panel, an axle step and a new plastic steering wheel all were standard for 1958.

Styling was basically the same, except for the two-tone hood color scheme. To speed up the manufacturing process, the yellow stripe on each side of the hood and the lettering were all on a decal.

Model 60

The Model 60 was introduced in June 1952. It was the successor to the great Model A, which had been on the market for 18 years. During that time, the A had gone through several evolutionary versions. The change to the Model 60 was revolutionary!

Completely new styling, like that of the Models R and M introduced in the previous years, was a departure from the styling first unveiled in 1938. Now there was a square hood with a bold new pleated grille.

The engine was the same displacement and configuration, and operated at the same 975 rpm as the A's engine, but improvements gave it more power, life and smoothness. Modified combustion chambers which increased intake turbulence, called "Cyclonic Fuel Intake," improved fuel-air mixing. Duplex carburetion, separate carburetor throats (gasoline versions, only at first) and passages kept pressure pulses of one cylinder from affecting the other. An intake heat riser valve reduced the possibility of carburetor icing.

Also new on the 60 was a positive crankcase ventilation system, an automatic fuel shut-off (controlled by oil pressure), a water pump, and thermostatically controlled radiator shutters, (replaced by a conventional thermostat and a pressurized radiator at S/N 6030927).

Other features included:
- A live PTO (optional).
- Powr-Trol with live hydraulics.
- Three-point hitch (optional).
- Power steering (1954).
- Rack and pinion rear wheel spacing.
- Two-piece pedestal allowing front end changes (optional until 1954).

Refinements to the 321-cid two-cylinder engine added 10 percent to the horsepower. This is the 1953 version of thee Model A. Owner: Marv Mathiowetz, Princeton, Minnesota

If the Model 60 had the two-piece pedestal, it could be converted between five fronts: Roll-O-Matic dual tricycle, dual tricycle without Roll-O-Matic, single front wheel, fixed 38in front tread, or the adjustable wide front end.
Owner: Rich Ramminger, Morrison, Wisconsin

- Optional rear exhaust.
- Optional long axles and dished wheels for 104 in. spacing.
- 12-volt electrical system.
- Improved seat.
- Longer clutch lever for easier operation when standing.

The Model 60 could be ordered in a host of different configurations. The most popular was the row-crop version. It could be ordered with five different front ends, or, if the tractor had the two-piece pedestal, it could be converted between the following five fronts:

- Roll-O-Matic dual tricycle.
- Dual tricycle without Roll-O-Matic.
- Single front wheel.
- Fixed 38 in. front tread.
- Adjustable wide front.

The Hi-Crop version was essentially a row-crop with the 38-inch fixed, or the adjustable wide front. It was higher giving a minimum of 32 inches of crop clearance.

Two versions of the standard-tread version were offered: the low-seat and the high-seat. The 60 low-seat was basically a slightly restyled and upgraded Model AR. Remember that the AR and AO production continued on until May 1953. At that point, the 60 low-seat carried on as a 1954 model.

The general acceptance of the larger Model 70 Standard, which was built on the row-crop chassis, led to a change at S/N 6043000. From then on, 60 Standards were built on row-crop frames as well, and the resultant dubbed the "high-seat standard."

The high-seat version could be ordered with an adjustable front axle. The 800 Series Yakima three-point hitch was also an option, as was power steering and LP gas fuel. Orchard Model 60s remained unchanged, except the LPG became available at S/N 6064000. Production of the 60 Orchard continued until February 1957 even though production of the other Model 60s ended in May 1956.

Model 60

Data and Specifications

Overall years built: 1952-1957
Overall serial numbers: 6000001-6064096
Number built: 61105
Built at: Waterloo, Iowa

Available Configurations:
Row Crop: Dual Tricycle Front/adjustable rear axle.
Adjustable Wide Front/adjustable rear axle.
Single Front Wheel/adjustable rear axle.
Adjustable long axles for 104 in spacing.
High Crop
Orchard
Low-seat Standard
High-seat Standard

Wheels/Tires
Front: 6.00-16 (dual, or wide front)
        7.50-16 or 9.00-10 (single front wheel)
Rear: 12.4/13.9-36
        11/12.4-38, 9/11-42

Length: 135 inches

Height (to top of hood): 65.6 inches

Weight: 5,900 lbs. (dual tricycle configuration)

Engine:
Type: Two-cylinder, four-stroke horizontal, side-by-side with pistons operating in opposition.
Bore & Stroke: 5.5 x 6.75 inches
Displacement: 321 cid
Rated RPM: 975 rpm
Compression Ratio:
    Gasoline: 6.08:1
    All-Fuel: 4.61:1
    LPG: 7.30:1

Carburetor
Gasoline: Marvel-Schebler DLTX-81
All-Fuel: Marvel-Schebler DLTX-72/84
LPG (S/N 6040105-6057649): John Deere AA6084R
(S/N 6057650 and up): John Deere AA6268R

Transmission:

Gear	Speed (mph)
1	1.50
2	2.50
3	3.50
4	4.50
5	6.25
6	11.00
Reverse	3.00

Price, New: $2,565 (1957)

Year Model vs Beginning Serial Number

Year	Beginning Serial Number
1952	6000001
1953	6004802
1954	6024786
1955	6039669
1956	60545000-6063853
1957	6063854-6064096 (orchard-only)

Row Crop

	First	Last
Gasoline	6000001	6063836
All-Fuel	6004878	6063787
LPG	6026000	6063853

Total Built: 57,166

High Crop

	First	Last
Gasoline	6000237	6062736
All-Fuel	6004825	6063357
LPG	6027468	6047932

Low-seat Standard

	First	Last
Gasoline	6025006	6042326
All-Fuel	6025243	6042732
LPG	none	

High-seat Standard

	First	Last
Gasoline	6043000	6063852
All-Fuel	6044024	6063673
LPG	6043841	6063384

Orchard

	First	Last
Gasoline	6025014	6064057
All-Fuel	6025371	6064096
LPG	6064000	6064095

In 1952, the Model A became the Model 60 with all the styling refinements characterizing the new two-number series. Standard features included rack and pinion rear wheel spacing, a 12-volt electrical system, an improved seat, and a longer clutch lever for easier operation when standing.
Owner: Marv Mathiowetz, Princeton, Minnesota

As early as 1953, the Deere New Generation tractors were in the works for introduction in 1960, but something would have to be done in the mean time. Marketing deemed the tractor line generally needed about 20 percent more horsepower per model–so the "Twenty Series" was conceived. The new 620 would be unveiled as a 1957 model replacing the Model 60.

Although the 620 looked like a 60 with yellow paint on the hood sides, it was changed considerably, especially in the engine. The 5.5-inch bore was retained, but that was the end of the similarities. The block, itself was completely new, with the spark plugs relocated to the cylinder heads. A drive pad for the distributor was provided so it would be driven by the camshaft, rather than by the governor gearing.

New cylinder heads provided a slightly higher compression ratio, and the sealing arrangement between the block and head was improved. The stroke was reduced .375 inches to 6.375 inches, for a displacement reduction from 321 to 303 cid. This displacement reduction was more than offset by an increase in operating speed from 975 rpm to 1125 rpm. Aluminum pistons, and beefed up rotating parts, along with combustion improvements, did indeed produce about 20 percent more horsepower. Fuel consumption was also improved.

Increased power dictated further changes:
- The final drives were strengthened.
- The PTO gears and clutch were strengthened.
- The front frame was strengthened and ballasted to maintain fore and aft balance.
- The fuel tank capacity was increased by almost two gallons.

The electrical system of this Model 620 has been converted to an alternator.
Owner: Ray Serr, Gregory, South Dakota

The 620 came out in 1956 and featured a draft-control three-point hitch and 20 percent more power than the Model 60 it replaced. Owner: Bruce Copper

A greatly improved Custom Powr-Trol completed the operational parts of the new tractor. Up to three separate hydraulic systems could be controlled from the operator's station. These included both front and rear rockshafts, three-point hitch (with top-link sensing draft control), or two separate remote cylinders.

The standard-tread version of the Model 620 could be called a "High-seat Standard" comparable to the High-seat 60, since it was made on the same frame as the row crop versions. Almost all of the options for the row crop versions were available for the standard-tread version, except the front rockshaft.

As noted previously, the 60 Orchard was essentially a restyled and upgraded Model AO. Production of the 60 Orchard continued past the retirement of the rest of the 60 line until May 1957. Again, only evolutionary changes were made to the 60 Orchard to make it into the 620 Orchard. These changes did include the new engine and driveline components. Interestingly, the 620 Orchard was continued after the 30 Series tractors were introduced until the end of the two-cylinder era in 1960.

Despite the extensive improvements made between the Model 60 and 620, the 1958 model saw an additional series of updates. Because the instrument panel was painted black, instead of green, these are now known as "Black Dash" 620s.

Changes included:
• Power adjustable rear wheel spacing (optional).
• Ball-joint tie rod ends for wide-front tractors.
• An improved muffler.
• Sealed beam headlights.
• Improved power steering (optional).
• A larger steering wheel.

The basic 620 was the row crop model in either gasoline or all-fuel versions. High-crop, Standard-tread and Orchard versions were priced $200 to $800 higher. The LP engine option added about $300. Other routinely supplied options were the Float-ride seat, a fuel gauge, power steering, live PTO, Custom Powr-Trol, adjustable wide-front axle, Roll-O-Matic, or single front wheel.

Model 620

Data and Specifications

Overall years built: 1957-1958 (Orchard model to1960)

Overall serial numbers: 6200000-6223247

Number built: 22532

Built at: Waterloo, Iowa

Available configurations:

Row Crop: Dual Tricycle Front/adjustable rear axle.

Adjustable Wide Front/adjustable rear axle. (*)

Single Front Wheel/adjustable rear axle. (*)

Adjustable long axles for 98 in. spacing.

Extra-long axles for up to 120 in. spacing.

(*)Std. equipment axle – 55 to 58 inches. The 1958 models with power adjustable wheel spacing are 56 to 94 inches of rear wheel spacing. Adjustable wide front is 48 to 80inches.

High Crop: Adjustable wide front/ adjustable rear axle – 55-58 inches.

Orchard : Tread spacing fixed, 55.5 inches.

Standard: Tread spacing fixed, 55.5 inches, 52-68 inches adjustable option front.

Wheels/Tires

Row Crop/High Crop

Front: 6.00-16 (dual, or wide front)
        7.50-20; 9.00-10 (single front wheel)

Rear: 11/12/12.4/13.6/15.5-38; 11-42

Standard Tread/Orchard

Front: 6.00-16, 6.50/7.50-18

Rear: 13/14/15-30

Length: 135 inches

Height (to top of hood): 66 inches

Weight: 5,900 lbs. (dual tricycle configuration)

Engine Type:

Two-cylinder, four-stroke horizontal, side-by-side with pistons operating in opposition.

Bore & stroke: 5.5 x 6.375 inches

Displacement: 302.9 cid

Rated RPM: 1125 rpm

Compression Ratio

Gasoline: 6.20:1

All-Fuel: 4.60:1

LPG: 8.10:1

Carburetor

Gasoline Row-crop (and Orchard to S/N 6222999): Marvel-Schebler DLTX-94

Gasoline Orchard (S/N 6223000 and up): Marvel-Schebler DLTX-106

All-Fuel: Marvel-Schebler DLTX-97

LPG: John Deere AA6821R

Electrical:

12-volts: ignition, starter and lights.

Transmission:

Gear	Speed (mph)
1	1.50
2	2.66
3	3.66
4	4.50
5	6.50
6	11.50
Reverse	3.00

Price, New: $2,650 (1958 Row Crop)

Year Model vs Serial Number

Year	Serial Number
1957	6200000-6213099
1958	6213100-6222686
1959	6223000-6223156 *
1960	6223157-6222686 *

* (Orchard-only)

Nebraska Test Data

Model 620 gasoline
Test Number 598
Date: 10-1956
Max. belt. hp.: 44.25
Max. drawbar pull lbs.: 6,122
Specific fuel consumption hp.-
    hrs./gal.: 12.52
Weight as tested (lbs.): 8,655

Model 620 distillate
Test Number 604
Date: 11-1956
Max. belt. hp.: 32.87
Max. drawbar pull lbs.: 6,107
Specific fuel consumption hp.-
    hrs./gal.: 11.25
Weight as tested (lbs.): 8,509

Model 620 LPG
Test Number 591
Date: 10-1956
Max. belt. hp.: 48.13
Max. drawbar pull lbs.: 5,920
Specific fuel consumption hp.-
    hrs./gal.: 9.6
Weight as tested (lbs.): 7,499

A row-crop gasoline version of the 620 is shown equipped with hydraulics, but no three-point hitch.
Owner: Ray Serr, Gregory, South Dakota.

Model 630

The Model 630 made its debut in August 1958 as a replacement for the Model 620. The emphasis of the Thirty Series was operator convenience, comfort and productivity. The 630 was the ultimate extension of the heritage of the original Model A, introduced in 1934.

According to Deere literature of the time, the 630 was capable of handling a four-bottom plow, or six-row planters and cultivators. The productivity of the 630 operator was easily double that of the original Model A.

The 630, and indeed the entire Thirty Series, almost didn't happen. The schedule for the New Generation John Deere tractors called for deliveries to begin in 1959. The Twenty Series tractors were to be the last of the Two-Cylinders. Shortly after the Twenty Series was unveiled, it became apparent the New Generation lineup would not be ready until late 1960. In an effort to keep

the New Generation line a secret from both customers and the competition, it was decided to put out the Thirty Series for the 1959 and 1960 model years.

The strategy was to give Henry Dreyfuss and Associates a free hand in modernizing the Twenty Series into the Thirty Series, without spending a lot of money on improving soon-to-be obsolete engines, transmissions and the like. The Dreyfuss industrial design team went to work to make the very good tractors of the Twenty Series even better.

As far as the 620 to 630 conversion was concerned, the designers concentrated on improving the comfort and convenience of the workstation. The most notable change was in the sharply angled steering wheel. The steering shaft was now almost completely beneath the engine hood. This new wheel position with the improved optional power steering, made control of the 630 second-to-none. Also, the new flat-top fenders protected the

The Model 630 was built from 1958 to 1960. It had the same power as the 620 it replaced, but with increased operator convenience and comfort, it was deemed more productive. Nearly 50 years old, it still looks good and is still working.
Owner: Daryl Hinderman, Dickeyville, Wisconsin

The standard –tread version of the 630 was available with gasoline, All-fuel, or LPG fuel systems. The one shown, a 1960 model, burns gasoline.
Owner: Maasdam Collection

This tractor has the optional Float-Ride seat with padded arm rests, power steering, Powr-Trol hydraulics with three-point hitch, pre-cleaner with air stack, and speed-hour meter.
Owner: Keller Collection

operator from dirt and debris, provided a convenient hand-hold for mounting and dismounting, and held a new four-light lighting system that better allowed for nighttime work.

Traditional clamshell fenders were also an option and generally used on standard tread versions. Finally, the workstation was completed with a proper instrument panel clustered around the steering wheel and a push-button starter.

Other improvements in the 630 were a new "Oval-Tone" muffler, an improved Float-Ride seat (optional), and a 1000rpm PTO option. The general styling was rounded-off somewhat, which gave the 630 a new look. The usual variations on the main row-crop theme were available, except for an Orchard model. Instead, a 620 Orchard, with some of the 630 improvements such as the push-button starter, soldiered on to the end.

Because performance factors were unchanged from the 620, the 630 did not require a Nebraska University test.

Model 630
Data and Specifications

Overall years built: 1959-1960
Overall serial numbers: 6300000-6318206
Number built: 18060
Built at: Waterloo, Iowa

Available configurations:

Row Crop: Dual Tricycle Front/adjustable rear axle (*)

Adjustable Wide Front/adjustable rear axle (*)

Single Front Wheel/adjustable rear axle (*)

Adjustable long axles for 62-98 in spacing (**)

Extra-long axles for up to 120 in spacing

(*)Std. Equipment axle – 55 to 58 inches. With power adjustable wheel spacing, 58 to 94 inches rear wheel spacing. Adjustable wide front, 48 to 80 inches. Standard and HD Roll-O-Matic, optional to dual tricycle.

(**) Dished wheels provided 58 to 104 inch spacing.

High Crop: Adjustable wide front/ adjustable rear axle – 55 to 58 inches

Standard: Tread spacing, 52 to 68 inches (adjustable front opt.)

Wheels/Tires
Row Crop/High Crop
Front: 6.00-16 (dual, or wide front)
　　　7.50-20; 9.00-10 (single front wheel)
Rear: 11/12/12.4/13.6/15.5-38; 11-42
Standard tread
Front: 6.00-16, 6.50/7.50-18
Rear: 14/15-30, 18.00-26 for industrial

Length: 135 inches

Height (to top of hood): 66 inches (dual tricycle configuration)

Weight: 5,900 lbs. (dual tricycle configuration)

Engine Type:

Two-cylinder, four-stroke horizontal, side-by-side with pistons operating in opposition.

Bore & Stroke:　　5.5 x 6.375 inches
Displacement:　　302.9 cid
Rated RPM:　　1125 rpm
Compression Ratio
　　Gasoline: 6.20:1
　　All-Fuel: 4.60:1
　　LPG: 8.10:1

Carburetor:

Gasoline Row-crop: Marvel-Schebler DLTX-94
All-Fuel : Marvel-Schebler DLTX-97
LPG: John Deere AA6821R

Electrical:

12-volts: ignition, starter and lights.

Transmission:

Gear	Speed (mph)
1	1.50
2	2.66
3	3.66
4	4.50
5	6.50
6	11.50
Reverse	3.00

Price, New: $2,955 (1959 Row Crop)

Year Model vs Serial Number

Year	Serial Number
1959	6300000-6312040
1960	6312041-6318206

Nebraska Test Data
Not Tested

The 630 had a relatively production short run, as it started in August, 1958 and ended in February, 1960.
Owner: Keller Collection

This row-crop version of the 630 has seen many hours of hard work over its nearly 50 years of service. The 630s are still much in demand by farmers because of their ability and durability.
Owner: Orv Rothgarn, Owatonna, Minnesota

The Model 70 made its debut a little later than its stable-mates, the 50 and 60, and it shared their features and styling. It was the successor to the great Model G, but was available in both standard-tread and row-crop configurations. It was also available in a variety of fuel choices besides the All-fuel (distillate) option. Power was up, for the 70 over the G, by almost 20 percent, even more for the fuel options other than distillate.

All engine options featured the new "raised eyebrow" over the intake valves to increase turbulence and fuel mixing, and the non-diesel types had the new duplex carburetor. The LPG option came out in 1954, while the new diesel appeared in 1955. The gasoline and LPG engines had a smaller bore diameter than the All-fuel engine, which was the same as that of the old Model G.

This was done to more-or-less equalize their power outputs in the 50 hp class. The diesel was also of a different displacement, with the same bore as the All-fuel engine, but with a shorter stroke for a higher rated operating speed than the others. The LP engine used aluminum pistons and a high-strength crankshaft because of the higher compression ratio. It also had exhaust valve rotators, and an extra set of gears in the distributor drive so the distributor would operate at half crankshaft speed (to prevent plug sparking on the exhaust stroke as is the case of other Deere two-cylinder engines). The diesel engine had a center main bearing for added stiffness.

The six-speed transmission was retained, although the 70 used the two-stick shift arrangement, while the other Deere tractors had been upgraded to the single

The Model 70 was offered in gasoline, LPG and All-fuel versions, but in 1954, a diesel was offered.
Owner: Marv Mathiowetz, Princeton, Minnesota.

The four-spoke steering wheel indicates that it is not equipped with power steering. This Model 70 has the gasoline engine and the non-Roll-O-Matic front end.
Owner: Marv Mathiowetz, Princeton, Minnesota

Three styles of the Model 70 were available: row-crop, standard and Hi-Crop. Four fuel types were options for all styles: gasoline, diesel All-fuel and LPG. The one shown is a wide-front Hi-Crop without power steering.
Owner: Pollock Collection

shift lever. Ratios were changed to give the diesel version the same travel speeds as the other engine types.

Standard equipment for row-crop tractors included a starter, belt pulley, PTO, lights, manual steering with a four-spoke steering wheel, thermostat cooling, swinging drawbar, a full-flow oil filter, a dual tricycle front end, Powr-Trol hydraulics, and either a gasoline or an All-fuel engine.

Options were power steering with a smaller three-spoke steering wheel, Roll-O-Matic or adjustable wide front end, single front wheel, Hi-crop equipment, live PTO, special rear axles and wheels, deluxe seat, fenders, tachometer/hour meter, rear exhaust, diesel or LPG

engines, and a cigarette lighter.

The standard-tread Model 70s came equipped much the same as the row-crops, except fenders were included in the base price. A fixed-tread front axle was also provided. Options for the Standard included most of those offered for the row-crops, except only an adjustable wide front axle was offered.

The Model 70 diesel recorded the lowest specific fuel consumption ever up to that time at the University of Nebraska, a remarkable achievement. This fact probably accounts in large measure for the popularity of the 70 diesel, which outsold the other versions by a two-to-one margin in the two years it was available.

Model 70
Data and Specifications

Overall years built: 1953-1956
Overall Serial Numbers: 7000001-7043757
Number built: 41,029
Built at: Waterloo, Iowa

Available Configurations:
Row Crop:
　Dual Tricycle Front/adjustable rear axle, 60 to 88 inches.
　Roll-O-Matic Front/ adjustable rear axle, 60 to 88 inches.
　Adjustable Wide Front, 56 to 80 inches/ adjustable rear axle, 60 to 88 inches.
　Single front wheel/adjustable rear axle, 60 to 88 inches.
　Adjustable long axles, 66 to 98 inches. (60 to 104 inches with dished wheels)
　Adjustable extra long axles, 66 to 106 inches (60 to 112 inches with dished wheels).
High Crop:
　Adjustable Wide Front, 60 to 84 inch /adjustable rear axle, 60 to 90 inches.
Standard Tread
　Fixed tread front axle, 55.5 inches
　Adjustable front axle, 52 to 68 inches.
　Adjustable rear axle, 62 to 80 inches.

Wheels/Tires
Row-Crop, Hi-Crop
　Front: 6.00-16 (dual, or wide front)
　　7.50-16 (single front wheel)
　　7.50-20 (Hi-Crop)
　Rear: 12/13-38
　Standard Tread
　Front: 6.50/7.50-18
　Rear: 14/15-30, 18-26

Length: 136 inches

Height: (to top of hood): 66 inches

Weight: 5,914 lbs. (Dual tricycle configuration)
　6,215 lbs. (Dual tricycle, LPG)
　6,305 lbs. (Dual tricycle, diesel)
　6,113 lbs. (Standard Tread)

Engine:
　Type: Two-cylinder, four-stroke horizontal, side-by-side with pistons operating in opposition.
　Gasoline and LPG:
　Bore & stroke: 5.875 x 7.00 inches
　Displacement: 379.5 cid
　Rated RPM: 975 rpm
　All-fuel:
　Bore & stroke: 6.125 x 7.00 inches
　Displacement: 412.5 cid
　Rated RPM: 975 rpm
　Diesel:
　Bore & Stroke: 6.125 x 6.375 inches
　Displacement: 375.6 cid
　Rated RPM: 1,125 rpm

Compression Ratio:
　Gasoline 6.15:1
　All-Fuel 4.60:1
　LPG 7.30:1
　Diesel 16.0:1

Diesel Starting Engine:
　Type: Four-cycle, four-cylinder, V-type, gasoline fuel, 6-volt electric starter
　Bore & Stroke: 2.00 x 1.50 inches
　Displacement: 18.85 cid
　Rated RPM: 5,500 rpm

Carburetor
　Gasoline: Marvel-Schebler DLTX-82
　All-Fuel: Marvel-Schebler DLTX-85
　LPG (S/N 7014800-7034949: John Deere AA6084R
　　(S/N 7034950 and up): John Deere AA6268R

Electrical: All, except diesel, 12-volt system with two batteries.
　Diesel, 6-volt, one battery

Transmission:

Gear	Speed (mph)
1	2.50
2	3.50
3	4.50
4	6.50
5	8.75
6	12.50
Reverse	3.25

Price, new: $2,855 (1954 basic row-crop tractor)
$2,750 (1956 basic standard-tread tractor)
Add: $675 for diesel option
$245 for LPG option

Year Model vs. Beginning Serial Number

Year	Beginning Serial Number
1953	7000001
1954	7002283
1955	7014803
1956	7031300

Nebraska Test Data

Model 70 gasoline
Test Number 493
Date: 5-1953
Max. belt. hp.: 50.35
Max. drawbar pull lbs.: 5,453
Specific fuel consumption hp.-hrs./gal.: 11.92
Weight as tested (lbs.): 8,647

Model 70 distillate
Test Number 506
Date: 9-1953
Max. belt. hp.: 44.96
Max. drawbar pull lbs.: 5,102
Specific fuel consumption hp.-hrs./gal.: 11.06
Weight as tested (lbs.): 8,155

Model 70 LPG
Test Number 514
Date: 11-1953
Max. belt. hp.: 51.97
Max. drawbar pull lbs.: 6,127
Specific fuel consumption hp.-hrs./gal.: 9.57
Weight as tested (lbs.): 8,950

Model 70 diesel
Test Number 528
Date: 10-1954
Max. belt. hp.: 51.49
Max. drawbar pull lbs.: 6,189
Specific fuel consumption hp.-hrs./gal.: 17.74
Weight as tested (lbs.): 9,017

The "cockpit" of a pony motor-start John Deere Model 70 diesel. The 70 was built between 1953 and 1956. This is a 1956 version.
Owner: Lyle Pals Collection

Model 720

The new Model 720 exhibited improvements in almost every area, especially in the engines. The non-diesel engines were entirely new with an almost square design. Their bore and stroke was almost equal at 6 x 6.375 inches. Operating speed was raised to 1,125 rpm, and that, along with other improvements, raised the horsepower by about 20 percent. For the first time, an oil dipstick was provided.

The displacement of the diesel engine was not changed, but changes to the pistons, enlarged intake valves and improved injectors gave 10 more horsepower.

The new diesel bested the fuel economy record set by its predecessor, the Model 70 diesel. It was a record that would stand for 30 years.

Another great improvement for the 720 was a single-lever shifter, replacing the two-stick type used on the Models G and 70. Gear ratios were also revised from those of the Model 70, with first gear now being a true "Creeper." In 1958, optional gears were offered that gave an eight-mile per hour fifth gear, and a six-mile per hour fourth.

Other improvements included larger brakes and

This LPG version of the Model 720 standard-tread was capable of 60 belt horsepower. New for the 720 was the load-compensating Custom Powr-Trol three-point hitch. The 720 was offered from 1956 through 1958.

improved power steering. Custom Powr-Trol now had "Load-and-Depth Control," a proper three-point hitch and provisions for two remote cylinders. Couplings for the remotes could be connected and disconnected under pressure without loosing fluid.

On tractors with manual steering, the pedestals were ballasted to weigh the same as front ends with power steering in order to retain the same fore/aft balance. The PTO now used a foot-pedal control with three positions: engaged, neutral and disengaged with a brake. The non-live (ground-driven) PTO option was eliminated.

A host of further improvements were made for the 1958 model year, but only one cosmetic one: the dash panel was now painted black. These are now known as "Black Dash" 720s and are preferred since so many minor refinements were incorporated.

Speaking of cosmetic changes, the Model 720 like the others in the Twenty Series, had a yellow stripe on the hood side panel. To save cost, this was a decal, rather than paint, since the labor required in masking would have been prohibitive.

Other options included:
- A rockshaft without a three-point hitch.
- A front rockshaft.
- A vertical air intake stack.
- A rearward exhaust.
- Electric fuel gauge (standard on diesels).

- Full foam seat cushion.
- Float Ride seat with foam rubber cushion.
- Fenders (standard on Standard Tread tractors).
- Speed-hour meter.
- Roll-O-Matic lock.
- Cigarette lighter.
- Power steering.
- High altitude pistons (for operation above 3000 msl).

There were some other changes between the 70 and 720 that were characteristic of the changes to the engines of other Waterloo Twenty series tractors. These included the relocation of the spark plug from the block to the cylinder heads. This change allowed for better combustion ignition and a higher compression ratio, especially with the All-fuel engine.

Higher compression and higher turning speed required more precise spark timing. Direct drive of the distributor from the camshaft eliminated the requirement for 2:1 reduction gearing, or firing of the plugs on the exhaust stroke (a problem for LPG engines) as had been done in the past.

Bypass starting was a technique used to get a hotter spark for starting by bypassing a resistor while the starter was engaged. When the starter pedal was released, the resistor was in the circuit, cutting the voltage to the distributor points in half, prolonging point life.

Enjoy the Greater Earning Power
of a *New* JOHN DEERE TRACTOR

The powerful new "720" Tractor with new, full-size, fully integral 4-bottom plow.

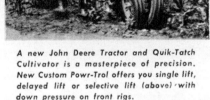

A new John Deere Tractor and Quik-Tatch Cultivator is a masterpiece of precision. New Custom Powr-Trol offers you single lift, delayed lift or selective lift (above) with down pressure on front rigs.

Good news travels fast! The new John Deere "520," "620," and "720" Tractors have put peak earning power on the farms of North America —with higher-than-ever standards for work output and ease of handling. Every day, more farmers are seeing these new 3-, 4-, and 5-plow tractors, driving them, and agreeing—with confidence and enthusiasm: "John Deere is the tractor for me." See your John Deere dealer and arrange for a free on-your-farm demonstration. Do it soon!

NEW More Powerful Engines. Completely re-designed combustion chamber provides increased power, smoother performance, and maximum fuel economy.

NEW CUSTOM Powr-Trol. An Advanced hydraulic system that offers as many as three independent hydraulic circuits for precision control of drawn, integral, and 3-point-hitch equipment.

NEW Universal 3-Point Hitch. Provides almost limitless adaptability and features exclusive Load-and-Depth Control to keep you on the move in varying ground conditions.

NEW Independent Power Take-Off. Delivers full engine horsepower, completely independent of the transmission clutch and hydraulic system.

NEW Float-Ride Seat. Absorbs shocks; makes rough fields seem smoother. Easily and accurately adjusted to operator's weight.

Advanced Power Steering. Smoother than ever; offers you new freedom from steering effort and driver fatigue every minute you're at the wheel.

Investigate the liberal John Deere Credit Plan— the easy, convenient means of paying for a new tractor while it earns profits for you.

6 Power Sizes... 30 Basic Models

Brian Rukes

Model 720
Data and Specifications

Overall years built: 1957-1958
Overall serial numbers: 7200000-7229002
Number built: 27,491
Built at: Waterloo, Iowa

Available configurations:
  Row Crop:
    Dual Tricycle Front (standard equipment):
    Non-adjustable wide-front, 38 inches
    Roll-O-Matic Front:
    Adjustable Wide Front, 56 to 80 inches
    Single Front Wheel:
    Adjustable rear axle, 60 to 88 inches
      (standard equipment).
    Adjustable long axles, 66 to 98 inches (60 to
      104 in with dished wheels).
    Adjustable extra long axles, 66 to 106 inches
      (60 to 112 inch with dished wheels.

  Hi-Crop
    Adjustable Wide Front, 60-84 in/adjustable
      rear axle, 60-90 inches

  Standard Tread:
    Fixed tread front axle, 55.5 inches
    Adjustable front axle, 52 to 68 inches
    Adjustable rear axle, 62 to 80 inches

Wheels/Tires
  Row-Crop, Hi-Crop
  Front: 6.00-16 (dual, or wide front)
    7.50-16 (single front wheel)
    7.50-20 (Hi-Crop)
  Rear: 12/13-38
  Standard Tread:
  Front: 6.50/7.50-18
  Rear: 14/15-30, 18-26

Length: 136 inches

Height (to top of hood): 66 inches

Weight: 6,030 lbs. (Dual tricycle configuration, gas)
    6,183 lbs. (Dual tricycle, LPG)
    6,533 lbs. (Dual tricycle, diesel, pony start)
    6,279 lbs. (Standard Tread, gas)

Engine:
  Type: Two-cylinder, four-stroke horizontal,
    side-by-side with pistons operating in
    opposition.

Gasoline, All-fuel and LPG:
Bore & Stroke: 6.00 x 6.375 inches
Displacement: 360.5 inches
Rated RPM: 1125 rpm

Diesel:
Bore & Stroke: 6.125 x 6.375 inches
Displacement: 375.6 cid
Rated RPM: 1,125 rpm
Compression Ratio
Gasoline 6.14:1
All-Fuel 4.91:1
LPG 7.30:1
Diesel 16.0:1
Diesel Starting Engine:
Type: Four-cycle, four-cylinder, V-type, gasoline
  fuel, 6-volt electric starter.
Bore & Stroke: 2.00 x 1.50 inches
Displacement: 18.85 cid
Rated RPM: 5,500 rpm

Carburetor:
  Gasoline: Marvel-Schebler DLTX-95
  All-Fuel: Marvel-Schebler DLTX-98   LPG
    John Deere AF2828R

Electrical: All, except diesel, 12-volt system with
  two batteries.
  Diesel, 6-volt, one battery.

Transmission:

Gear	Speed (mph)
1	1.50
2	2.25
3	3.50
4	4.50
5	5.75
6	11.50
Reverse	3.25

Price, new: $3,190 (1958 basic row-crop tractor)
               $3,410 (1958 basic standard-tread
                         tractor)
Add: $750 for diesel option
          $295 for LPG option

Year Model vs Beginning Serial Number

Year	Beginning Serial Number
1957	7200000
1958	7214900-7229001 (last)

S/N 7215262 was rebuilt and sold as S/N 7229002

Nebraska Test Data

Model 720 gasoline
Test Number 605
Date: 11-1956
Max. belt. hp.: 59.12
Max. drawbar pull lbs.: 6,647
Specific fuel consumption hp.-hrs./gal.: 12.21
Weight as tested (lbs.): 8,945

Model 720 distillate
Test Number 606
Date: 11-1956
Max. belt. hp.: 45.33
Max. drawbar pull lbs.: 6,608
Specific fuel consumption hp.-hrs./gal.: 10.89
Weight as tested (lbs.): 8,985

Model 720 LPG
Test Number 593
Date: 9-1956
Max. belt. hp.: 59.61
Max. drawbar pull lbs.: 6,664
Specific fuel consumption hp.-hrs./gal.: 9.27
Weight as tested (lbs.): 9,061

Model 720 diesel
Test Number 594
Date: 9-1956
Max. belt. hp.: 58.84
Max. drawbar pull lbs.: 6,547
Specific fuel consumption hp.-hrs./gal.: 17.97
Weight as tested (lbs.): 9,297

The John Deere Model 730 was the ultimate two-cylinder row-crop. Strong, stylish, economical and as modern for the time as you will find. Possibly the only weak point in the use of the tractor 40-plus-years later is only six forward speeds and one reverse were provided.

Even during the time when the 730 was new, it was as good or better than the competition in every area except transmission speeds. This minor deficiency was more than offset by its reliability, the strength and stability of its dealers, and its fuel economy.

Some argue effectively that the broad torque curve of the long-stroke two-cylinder engine made up for the lack of transmission gears, or of a power shift auxiliary device (Torque Amplifier).

The 730 tractors debuted in August of 1958 as 1959 models. As early as the fall of 1957, Deere product planners knew the New Generation tractors would not be ready to come out as 1959 models, but would need further development that would carry the introduction date well into 1960.

It was also known that Harvester, Case, Massey Ferguson, Cockshutt, Minneapolis-Moline, Oliver and Ford would all be introducing tractors in the 60 horsepower class by the time the New Generation tractors would be ready. The planners concluded that something had to be done to make the Model 720 (and other Twenty Series tractors) appear to be new models for 1959.

What looked as though Deere had gotten itself into a competitive box, turned out to be an opportunity in disguise. Henry Dreyfuss and Associates were called in and told to make the Thirty Series look competitive and as though the two-cylinder tractor was to be offered for the foreseeable future. The Dreyfuss team accomplished the goal of making the tractor seem a viable competitor. Whether or not the competition believed the two-cylinder engine ruse is now a moot point.

Model 730 tractors were made in Row-crop, Hi-crop and Standard-tread versions, the same as the 720. The same engine options were also offered. Since the basic tractors were unchanged from their 720 counterparts,

This Model 730 row-crop was powered by a 360.5-cid two-cylinder gasoline engine. Deere built 3560 of these as 1959 and 1960 models.
Owner: Ken Kass, Dunkerton, Iowa

This Model 730 row-crop tractor has the optional Roll-O-Matic front end.
Owner: Ken Kass, Dunkerton, Iowa

terminated in February 1960. The last domestic 730 was shipped in June 1960, but production continued for export to March 1961.

Deere had set up a production facility in Rosario, Argentina, to build 730s from parts shipped from Waterloo, Iowa. When production ended in Waterloo, tooling was shipped to Rosario and total Argentine production continued to sometime in 1968.

Argentine tractors were Row-crop, Hi-crop and Standard, but all were electric-start diesels. About 20,000 were produced. Kit production of 730s also took place in Monterrey, Mexico, during the 1959 and 1960 model years. Most were Row-crop diesels. Factory records only indicate the serial number blocks assigned to Mexican production, not how many, or of what types these tractors were.

no testing was required at the University of Nebraska in order to sell the Model 730 in Nebraska.

Possibly the only change between the two, other than in the areas of styling and ergonomics, was a rack-and-pinion adjustable rear axle was provided for the 730 Hi-crop. Operators of these tractors desired to use 18.4-34 rear tires to get better traction and flotation, but the larger tires interfered with structure. A short stub axle was designed that could readily accommodate the necessary wheel adjustment.

Standard equipment and options for the 730 were much the same as for the 720. Ergonomic changes resulted in the new flat top fenders with integral lights being offered as an option. These fenders had hand-holds that greatly helped in mounting and dismounting. Ergonomics also dictated the new, more comfortable steering wheel position. Not so strangely, these two features would find there way into the New Generation tractors.

The 730 was in such demand that production continued after the rest of the Thirty Series were

The Float-Ride seat improved the ride for the drivers of the Model 730 row-crop tractor.
Owner: Ken Kass, Dunkerton, Iowa

Model 730
Data and Specifications

Overall years built: 1958-1961
Overall serial numbers: 7300000-7330358
Number built: 29,713 (Waterloo only)
Built at: Waterloo, Iowa – Monterrey, Mexico – Rosario, Argentina

Available configurations:
Row Crop:
    Dual Tricycle Front (standard equipment)
    Non-adjustable wide-front, 38 inches
    Roll-O-Matic Front
    Adjustable Wide Front, 56 to 80 inches
Single Front Wheel:
    Adjustable rear axle, 60 to 88 inches (standard equipment)
    Adjustable long axles, 66 to 98 inches (60 to 104 inches with dished wheels)
    Adjustable extra long axles, 66 to 106 inches (60 to 112 inches with dished wheels).
Hi-Crop:
    Adjustable Wide Front, 60 to 84 inches/ adjustable rear axle, 60 to 90 inches.
Standard Tread:
    Fixed tread front axle, 55.5 inches
    Adjustable front axle, 52 to 68 inches
    Adjustable rear axle, 62 to 80 inches

Wheels/Tires
    Row-Crop, Hi-Crop:
    Front: 6.00-16 (dual, or wide front)
        7.50-16 (single front wheel)
        7.50-20 (Hi-Crop)
    Rear: 12/13-38
    Standard tread:
    Front: 6.50/7.50-18
    Rear: 14/15-30, 18-26

Length: 136 inches

Height (to top of hood): 66 inches

Weight: 6,030 lbs. (Dual tricycle configuration, gas)
    6,183 lbs. (Dual tricycle, LPG)
    6,533 lbs. (Dual tricycle, diesel, pony start)
    6,279 lbs. (Standard Tread, gas)

Engine:
Type: Two-cylinder, four-stroke horizontal, side-by-side with pistons operating in opposition.
Gasoline, All-fuel and LPG:
Bore & stroke: 6.00 x 6.375 inches
Displacement: 360.5 cid
Rated RPM: 1125 rpm
Diesel:
Bore & Stroke: 6.125 x 6.375 inches
Displacement: 375.6 cid
Rated RPM: 1,125 rpm
Compression Ratio:
Gasoline 6.14 :1
All-Fuel 4.91:1
LPG 7.30:1
Diesel 16.0:1
Diesel Starting Engine:
Type: Four-cycle, four-cylinder, V-type, gasoline fuel, 6-volt electric starter.
Bore & Stroke: 2.00 x 1.50 inches
Displacement: 18.85 cid
Rated RPM: 5,500 rpm

Carburetor:
Gasoline: Marvel-Schebler DLTX-95
All-Fuel: Marvel-Schebler DLTX-98
LPG: John Deere AF2828R

Electrical: All, except diesel, 12-volt system with two batteries.
    Diesel, 6-volt, one battery.

Transmission:

Gear	Speed (mph)
1	1.50
2	2.25
3	3.50
4	4.50
5	5.75
6	11.50
Reverse	3.25

Price, New: $3,190 (1958 basic row-crop tractor)

$3,410 (1958 basic standard-tread tractor)

Add: $750 for diesel option

$295 for LPG option

Year Model vs. Beginning Serial Number

(Does not include Argentinian production)

Year	Beginning Serial Number
1959	7300000
1960	7318180
1961	7329300-7330358

Serial Number Blocks Assigned to Mexican Production:

7300600-7300739

7304000-7304109

7307000-7307110

7310100-7310163

7316200-7316254

7320200-7320239

Nebraska Test Data

Model 730 gasoline

Test Number 605

Date: 11-1956

Max. belt. hp.: 59.12

Max. drawbar pull lbs.: 6,647

Specific fuel consumption hp.-hrs./gal.: 12.21

Weight as tested (lbs.): 8,945

Model 730 distillate

Test Number 606

Date: 11-1956

Max. belt. hp.: 45.33

Max. drawbar pull lbs.: 6,608

Specific fuel consumption hp.-hrs./gal.: 10.89

Weight as tested (lbs.): 8,985

Model 730 LPG

Test Number 593

Date: 9-1956

Max. belt. hp.: 59.61

Max. drawbar pull lbs.: 6,664

Specific fuel consumption hp.-hrs./gal.: 9.27

Weight as tested (lbs.): 9,061

Model 730 diesel

Test Number 594

Date: 9-1956

Max. belt. hp.: 58.84

Max. drawbar pull lbs.: 6,547

Specific fuel consumption hp.-hrs./gal.: 17.97

Weight as tested (lbs.): 9,297

The Dubuque tractors had grown to be a little expensive for some truck gardeners and tobacco farmers. In the summer of 1956, a new bottom-of-the-line small tractor was unveiled: the Model 320. The 320 was offered in two configurations: the Standard and the Utility. The Standard had a crop clearance of 21 inches and was a favorite with farmers. The Utility model was about 5 inches lower in overall height, and appealed to fruit growers, highway mowers and those using the tractor in restricted places.

The 320 was a conglomerate of more-or-less existing tractor parts. The engine was essentially that of the old Model 40 with the speed reduced to 1,650 rpm. The transmission came from the M. Final drives were the same as early versions of the 40 Standard and Utility. The balance of the 320 shared sheet metal, hydraulics, axles and steering, with the Model 420.

Both gasoline and All-fuel (distillate) engines were offered, although very few of the "kerosene burners" were sold.

The styling features of the Twenty Series tractors were carried over to the 320. For the 1958 model year (which started at a new "round" serial number), a slanted steering wheel replaced the old vertical wheel. The Model 420 received this change, and since parts were shared, the 320 got it also.

Standard equipment for both the 320S and 320U included fenders, starter, adjustable seat, single Touch-O-Matic hydraulics, three-point hitch, and adjustable-tread axles. Options included the All-fuel engine, lights, underneath exhaust, dual Touch-O-Matic hydraulics, PTO, belt pulley, foot throttle, and high-altitude pistons.

The 320 was also sold in a configuration known as a Southern Special, or 320V. These tractors were special order from the factory and had 10-34 rear tires along with front axle, fenders and hitch of the 420 Special (V).

Records of these "Specials" are sketchy, at best, so not much else is known about them. They are not in any respect low-cost tractors today!

These tractors were a special order from the factory and had 10-34 rear tires along with front axle, fenders and hitch of the 420 Special (V). Owner: Keller Collection

The Model 320 was sold in a configuration known as a Southern Special, or 320V.
Owner: Keller Collection

Model 320
Data and Specifications

Overall years built: 1957-1958
Serial numbers: 320001-325518
Number built: 3,084
Built at: Dubuque, Iowa

Model 320U
Configuration: Utility
Number built:
    Straight-steer gasoline: 716
    Straight-steer All-fuel: 2
    Slant-steer gasoline: 199
    Slant-steer All-fuel: 0

Wheels/Tires:
    Front: 5.00 x 15
    Rear: 9/10 - 24

Transmission: 4-speed
Speeds: 1.63, 3.12, 4.25, 12.0 mph (9-24 rears)
Reverse: 1.62 mph
Axles:
    Front, Adjustable: 43-55 inches
    Rear, Adjustable: 41-56 inches
Shipping weight: 2,674 lbs.
Price, new: $1,885

Model 320S
Configuration: Standard
Number built:
    Straight-steer gasoline: 1,836
    Straight-steer All-fuel: 12
    Slant-steer gasoline: 317
    Slant-steer All-fuel: 2

Wheels/Tires:
    Front: 5.00 x 15
    Rear: 9/10 - 24

Transmission: 4-speed
Speeds: 1.63, 3.12, 4.25, 12.0 mph (9-24 rears)
Reverse: 1.62 mph
Axles:
    Front, Adjustable: 40-55 inches
    Rear, Adjustable: 39-54 inches
Shipping weight: 2,657 lbs.
Price, new: $1,805

Engine:
    Type: Vertical two-cylinder, with pistons operating in opposition.
    Bore & Stroke: 4.00 x 4.00 inches
    Displacement: 100.54 cid
    Rated RPM: 1650
    Fuel: gasoline or distillate
    Compression Ratio: 6.50:1 gasoline
                                  4.70:1 distillate
    Ignition: coil, 6-volt
    Cooling: thermosyphon
    Carburetor:
        Gasoline: Marvel-Schebler TSX-245
        All-fuel: Marvel-Schebler TSX-475

Serial Numbers vs. Year Model

Designation	Serial Numbers	Year
Straight-steer	320001-322566	1957
Slant-steer	325001-325518	1958

Serial Numbers 322567-325000 were not used

Nebraska Test Data
Not tested

The Model 320 used the 4x4, 100.5-cid engine running at 1650rpm.
Owner: Keller Collection

Model 330

The Model 330 was introduced along with the rest of the Thirty Series John Deere tractor lineup in August 1958 as a 1959-year model. Essentially, it was the same as its predecessor, the Model 320, with the same two variations: the 330U (Utility) and the 330S (Standard).

There were some significant improvements, besides the attractive Dreyfuss styling job. The most important was the relocation of the oil filler/breather from the valve cover to the engine block, and the addition of a proper dipstick. This addition was long overdue on Deere tractors! Another new feature was a slanted, easy-to-read instrument panel. The All-fuel option was not carried over from the 320. The illusive 330V (Southern Special) high-clearance version did continue as a special-order item. Apparently, only about 25 left the factory for Louisiana, Texas and Mississippi.

Options and standard equipment were essentially the same for the 330 as for the 320, except hydraulics was no longer standard on the Utility model. This was because many buyers of that version did not need the hydraulic system and didn't want to pay for it.

The newly formed Industrial Division (established in 1956) sold 330s, but they were not different from those sold by the regular dealer network, except for varieties of Highway colors. Nor were they were identified with a different serial number sequence, but some did have different lettering on the sides, and of course, no yellow side decals.

The last 330 was built in February 1960. The line was then converted to production of the New Generation tractors. It was the last of Deere's truly small farm tractors and the culmination of the line that started with the diminutive Model L back in 1937.

As with small cars, the problem is not in making them small, but in getting the price down to where they cost less than a larger, more capable machine. The 320 and 330 did quite well at this, being between $100 and $200 less than the 420/430 models due to the fact that they used a variety of more-or-less existing parts with costs already sunk for these parts.

The Model 330 had evolved from the Model M of 1947, a design developed during World War II, but not produced. By the end of the war, it was obvious the Ford-Ferguson, brought out in 1939 and built through the war years, was winning the hearts and minds of the small-acreage farmer. Ford had been averaging sales of 42,000 of the little gray tractors per year during the war. The new John Deere M, it was hoped, would stem Ford's tide and garner its share of the small tractor market.

Sales of the M, MT and MC tractors averaged about 14,000 per year from 1947 to 1952. Besides the Ford (which was probably more in competition with the John Deere B on the basis of price and weight), others were competing for the small tractor market. International, Allis-Chalmers, Massey-Harris, Case and soon Ferguson (after the split with Ford) were all after a share of this market. Strangely, at this time the market started disappearing in favor of more powerful and more expensive tractors. The Models M, 40, 420 and 430 from John Deere performed admirably and stood up well against the best the competition offered.

The Model 330 had two-cylinder 100.5 cid engine with ample power to pull two 12-inch bottoms. It was available for gasoline fuel, only.
Owner: Don Wolf, Ft. Wayne, Indiana

Overall years built: 1959-1960
Serial numbers: 330001-331091
Number built: 1,091
Built at: Dubuque, Iowa

Model 330U
Configuration: Utility
Number built: 247

Wheels/Tires:
    Front: 5.00 x 15
    Rear: 9/10 - 24

Transmission: 4-speed
Speeds: 1.62, 3.12, 4.25, 12.0 mph (9-24 rears)
Reverse: 1.62 mph
Axles:
    Front, Adjustable: 43-55 inches
    Rear, Adjustable: 41-56 inches
Shipping weight: 2,684 lbs.
Price, new: $2,200

Model 330S
Configuration: Standard
Number built: 844

Wheels/Tires:
    Front: 5.00 x 15
    Rear: 9/10 - 24

Transmission: 4-speed
Speeds: 1.62, 3.12, 4.25, 12.0 mph (9-24 rears)
Reverse: 1.62 mph
Axles:
    Front, Adjustable: 40-55 inches
    Rear, Adjustable: 39-54 inches

Shipping weight: 2,667 lbs.
Price, new: $2,105

Engine:
    Type: Vertical two-cylinder, with pistons
        operating in opposition.
    Bore & stroke: 4.00 x 4.00 inches
    Displacement: 100.54 cid

Rated RPM: 1650
Fuel: gasoline
Compression Ratio: 6.50:1
Ignition: coil, 6-volt
Cooling: thermosyphon
Carburetor: Marvel-Schebler TSX-245

Serial Numbers vs. Year Model

Serial Numbers	Year
330001 - 330814	1959
330815 – 331091	1960

Nebraska Test Data
Not tested

"Colossal," is the term that comes to mind when an 8010/8020 comes into view. Even today, when the very large tractors are everywhere, the 8010/8020 still has a commanding presence. One can only imagine the awe that it inspired when first introduced in 1959 (and the 830 was the big tractor then in everyone's imagination). Why mention the 8010 and 8020 together? Actually, they are mostly one and the same. Of the one hundred 8010s built, all but a few were rebuilt into 8020s.

Deere was hard at work on the New Generation tractors at the same time that the 8010 was in its prototype stage. Recognizing that production of this big tractor would be low, Deere made use of existing components where possible. One such item was the engine. Deere had had recent experience with Detroit Diesel engines in the much-smaller Model 435. The General Motors Detroit Diesel unit had pioneered the modular 2-cycle diesels. They had already been on the market for a number of years, notably as locomotive power plants.

There were several sizes of piston displacement to choose from including 53 cid per cylinder to over 100 cid per cylinder. Since the engines were of the 2-cycle type, the customer could specify the number of cylinders they wanted to get the necessary horsepower. The 2-53 engine of the Model 435 had 2 cylinders of 53 cubic inches of displacement each, or 106 total cid. Since it was a 2-cycle engine, with one power stroke per revolution per cylinder, its power output was more like that of a four. Also inherent with the 2-cycle engine was it sounded like it was turning twice as fast as it really was. The 8010/8020 would use the 6-71 engine with 71 cid per cylinder or 426 cid, total.

The GM engine used only exhaust valves. Intake air arrived pressurized by a Rootes-type blower through ports in the sides of the cylinder wall. When the piston traveled down, the exhaust valve opened and the piston uncovered the ports. Pressurized air from the blower rushed in, purging the exhaust gasses through

Deere's first over-200 horsepower tractor was the giant Model 8010, which came in at 215 hp.
Owner: Keller Collection

Deere's first over-200 horsepower tractor was the giant Model 8010, which came in at 215 hp.
Owner: Keller Collection

the exhaust valve. As the piston started up, the ports were covered and the exhaust valve closed. Near the top of the stroke, fuel was injected. Auto ignition of the fuel, due to the heat of compression, started the piston downward, and the cycle started over again. Although the blower provided some supercharging, its purpose was to expel the burnt gasses and introduce fresh air for the next cycle.

As originally built, the 8010 used a 9-speed truck transmission that mated nicely with the Detroit 6-71 diesel (also commonly used in trucks). Unfortunately, the transmission overheated with tractor loads and speeds, causing seals to go out and transmission oil to get on the clutch. Once this happened, it was time for an expensive rebuild.

The first post-prototype 8010 was built in June of 1960, and the last in March of 1961. In November of 1963, the first of those, S/N 1041, was made into an 8020. Those that had been sold were recalled, rebuilt and returned to their owners as 8020s. Others that had not been sold were converted, and a supreme effort made to find buyers for them. Records show the last one was not sold until 1965, or perhaps, later. Some found their way into John Deere's "permanent" inventory, to be used around the factory farms and yards and later sold as used.

The 8010/8020 was a useful piece of equipment, although at nearly $30,000 in the early 1960s, a farmer had to expect to retire four or five lesser tractors (and drivers) to justify the expense. When rebuilt to be an 8020, the tractor had the New Generation seat and was quite up to John Deere standards of ergonomics. For example, when the headlights were on, step lights and a toolbox light also came on.

The big tractor could be equipped with a class five three-point hitch. Dual hydraulic systems were standard, and of course, power steering, through the pivot cylinder that controlled articulation, was standard. A hydraulically actuated clutch was easily operated by the lightest driver. Air brakes were provided that were well capable of stopping the monster from its 18 mph-road speed. The air system could also be used to inflate tires, or for air tools.

A notable feature was a single-point lubrication panel, where most items requiring the services of a grease gun could be greased at this convenient panel. For road operation, the front wheel drive could be disengaged.

Most 8010/8020s left the factory in green and yellow livery, but some were sold in industrial yellow. Almost all were sold without cabs, but cabs were added to some later.

Overall years built: 1959-1964

Built at: Waterloo, Iowa

Available configuration: Articulated four-wheel drive

Wheels/Tires:
Front and Rear: 23.1-26, 20 in wide rims

Engine:
General Motors-built Detroit Diesel 6-71, inline six-cylinder diesel, overhead exhaust valves, two-cycle, Rootes blower scavenged
Bore & Stroke: 4.25 x 5.00 inches
Displacement: 426 cid
Rated RPM: 2100 rpm
Compression Ratio: 17:1
Cooling: Thermostat and pump

Starter: 24-Volt Direct Electric Starting, four 6-volt batteries (other electrical functions, 12-volts)

Transmission: 8010, 9-speed
8020, 8-speed
Travel speeds 2.0 to 18 mph

Weight: 20,700 – 24,860 lbs.

Length: 19 ft.-7 inches

Width: 8.0"

Height: 9 ft.-6 inches (to top of air cleaner)

Price, New: $30,500 with 3-point hitch

Nebraska Test Data
Not tested

Engine rated horsepower – 215 @ 2100rpm
Drawbar horsepower (Mfr. Est.) - 150

Model 8010/8020 Serial Numbers

Year	First
1960	1000 (about 100 built)
1964	1000 (rebuilt 8010s)

A new type transmission was used with four speeds forward and a two-speed auxiliary.
Owner: Paul Kleiber, Plymouth, Wisconsin

The Dubuque Tractor works had been building tractors with vertical in-line engines for four years in 1953 when word came the entire Deere tractor line would be modernized. The target introduction year was 1961, (the Fall of 1960). The two-cylinder engines would be replaced with engines of more than two-cylinders. The Waterloo-built tractors would now be of a similar configuration to the Dubuque tractors with vertical in-line (with the tractor's centerline) engines. Dubuque's Chief Engineer Willard Nordenson did not face the major challenges faced by the Waterloo engineers. His job consisted mainly of adapting new engines to their existing line of small tractors and of incorporating in them the new styling themes coming from the Dreyfuss studios.

Two new four-cylinder engines, a gasoline and a diesel, would be developed. The gasoline engine was actually introduced in 1959 as a power plant for a self-propelled combine. Dubuque had been making four-cylinder engines for some time for Deere harvesters. The

gasoline engine would displace 115 cubic inches, while the diesel would displace 145 cid. The diesel would be of the glow-plug start variety.

Prototypes of the tractor that would become the Model 1010 were available for testing as early as 1955. The search for more profits prompted the company to trim the number of models and options and to make the industrial line share more with the agricultural tractors. Dubuque sales had been greatly boosted by deliveries of yellow (industrial) machines. Therefore, most of the early 1010s were for the industrial market. The first agricultural Model 1010 was a crawler, the 107th 1010 built.

The 1010s were introduced to the public, along with the rest of the New Generation tractors, on Aug. 30, 1960 at Deere Day in Dallas, Texas. Dealers from all over the country were flown to Dallas for the grand unveiling of the new tractor line. It was a great marketing triumph for Deere, and both dealers and customers responded favorably to the new offerings despite loyalty to the two-cylinder line that extends to this day.

The Model 1010 was the smallest of the new generation tractors. It was marketed from 1960 to 1965. For the 1962 model year, a grove, or orchard tractor was added to the line. It was not much different from the Utility version, except for the skirted rear fenders.

The Model 1010 (O) offered a five-speed transmission and either a gasoline, or diesel engine. A live PTO and a Float Ride seat were options, as was a dual remote hydraulic system. The one shown has a gasoline engine.

The new 1010 offered a five-speed transmission for wheel types and a four-speed for crawlers. Originally, the shift control was located on the dash. Later, it was moved back to the transmission top due to linkage problems. A live PTO and a Float Ride seat were options, as was a dual remote hydraulic system.

For 1962, a grove, or orchard tractor was added to the line. It was not much different from the Utility version, except for the skirted rear fenders.

The 1963 model year began with serial number 31001 to indicate some more major changes. First was the relocation of the shift lever. The final drive was strengthened and given a higher numeric ratio to improve drawbar pull. Other improvements, especially to the diesel engine, were also made, including a primer to help with cold weather starting.

A lower-cost version of the Row Crop Utility was offered, called the Special Row Crop Utility, with a plain seat and few options. It sold for about $300 less and was popular on factory farms where operators were hired, and were not owner-operators. A tricycle option for the row crop version also came out in 1963 with dual narrow, or single, front wheels. Roll-O-Matic was

available with the dual narrow front. This version used 36-inch rear wheels and a revised final drive.

When Henry Ford and Harry Ferguson pooled their talents in 1939 and produced a small, light, inexpensive tractor with a three-point hitch, the gurus of the full-line implement companies at first, ignored them.

After World War II, the gurus discovered an important segment of the market was not being adequately covered by their line up of models. Deere was among the first to react with the Model M in 1947. Ford and Ferguson had a falling out in that year and went their separate ways (giving Deere two competitors, instead of one). Deere improved its offering and competitive position almost every year, as did Ford and Ferguson.

In 1955, Ferguson merged with Massey Harris to become Massey Ferguson. By 1960, when the John Deere 1010 was introduced, it featured a three-point hitch with load and depth control, and a smooth running four-cylinder engine, it was the one to beat. (See comparison table below.) The Deere had a competitive price and 10 industrial and agricultural variations to choose from.

Model 1010
Data and Specifications

Overall Years Built: 1961-1965
Built at: Dubuque, Iowa

Available configurations:
- row crop (R)
- row crop utility (RU)
- utility (U)
- Special Row Crop Utility (RUS)
- single row crop (RS)
- grove/orchard (O)
- ag crawler (CA)
- high crop (H)*

(Letters in parentheses are stamped with serial numbers.)
*Records indicate only one built.

Wheels/Tires
Front: 5.00-15 standard,   6.00-16 optional
Rear: 10-34 standard,   12-28 optional

Engine Options:

Gasoline
Number of cylinders: 4
Bore & stroke: 3.5 x 3 inches
Displacement: 115.5 cid
Rated RPM: 2,500
Cooling: Pump

Diesel
Number of cylinders: 4
Bore & stroke: 3.625 x 3.5 inches
Displacement: 144.5 cid
Rated RPM: 2,500
Cooling: Pump

Transmission:

Gear	Speed (mph)
Crawler	
1	1.4
2	1.93
3	3.32
4	6.5
Wheel	
1	2.62
2	3.50
3	4.75
4	8.78
5	16.86

Shipping weight:

Wheel tractor	3,923 lbs.
Crawler	7,580 lbs.

Price, new:

Wheel tractors	$2,130-$2,350
Crawler	$1,866-$1,950
Diesel option	$ 500
Live PTO	$ 115

Nebraska Test Data

Model 1010RU Gas
Test Number 802
Date: 6-1961
Max. belt. hp.: 36.13
Max. available drawbar hp.*: 30.00
Specific fuel consumption hp.-hrs./gal.: 10.33
Weight as tested (lbs.): 5,711

Model 1010RU Diesel
Test Number 803
Date: 6-1961
Max. belt. hp.: 35.99
Max. available drawbar hp.*: 29.16
Specific fuel consumption hp.-hrs./gal.: 11.93
Weight as tested (lbs.): 5,754

Model 1010C Gas
Test Number 801
Date: 6-1961
Max. belt. hp.: 35.93
Max. available drawbar hp.*: 7,179
Specific fuel consumption hp.-hrs./gal.: 11.35
Weight as tested (lbs.): 7,370

Model 1010C Diesel
Test Number 798
Date: 6-1961
Max. belt. hp.: 36.31
Max. available drawbar hp.*: 7,484
Specific fuel consumption hp.-hrs./gal.: 13.84
Weight as tested (lbs.): 7,580

*At the beginning of the 1959 testing season, changes were made in the way drawbar power was assessed. Rather than maximum low gear drawbar pull, maximum available drawbar horsepower was recorded. This was based on a combination of pull and speed. For these crawlers, however, maximum low gear pull was recorded. Also at the beginning of 1959, belt power testing was discontinued in favor of PTO testing.

Comparisons

Make/model	Cylinders	Displacement	PTO hp	Drawbar hp	Test weight
Deere 1010D	4	145 cid	36	29	5,754lbs
Ford 681D	4	144 cid	32	26	5,485lbs
Massey F 135D	3	153 cid	37	32	5,780lbs

Model Variations: First and Last Serial Numbers and Build Dates

Model	First/Last	Gasoline Serial No.	Build date	Diesel Serial No.	Build Date
IndustrialCrawler (C)	First	10001	6-01-60	10835	8-01-60
	Last	52977	11-17-64	52971	11-17-64
AgriculturalCrawler (CA)	First	10108	6-15-60	10948	8-04-60
	Last	52320	10-14-64	52703	10-30-64
Single Row Crop (RS)	First	10309	7-08-60	10903	8-02-60
	Last	57280	9-24-65	56820	7-19-65
Row Crop Utility (RU)	First	15054	12-22-60	15297	1-11-61
	Last	57312	9-29-65	52310	9-29-65
Utility (U)	First	10763	7-28-60	10901	8-12-60
	Last	57269	9-24-65	56759	7-14-65
Orchard (O)	First	24402	11-30-61	25583	11-15-62
	Last	54510	2-17-65	52811	11-03-64
Industrial Wheel (W)	First	10381	7-12-60	15295	1-10-61
	Last	57287	9-24-64	57296	9-27-65
Row Crop (R)	First	37002	4-02-63	37011	4-02-63
	Last	57301	9-28-65	57275	9-24-65

Note: Special row crop (RUS) figures are included in row crop (R)

Model 1010 Serial Number Vs Year Model

Year	Beginning Serial Number
1961	10001
1962	21883
1963	31001
1964	42001
1965	50917

Last Serial Number – 57312

The Model 1020 replaced the 1010 line in 1965. Only three versions were offered, rather than the 1010's eight versions. The 1020 was one of the first of the "Worldwide" tractors from Deere, and was therefore more along the lines of tractors popular in other parts of the world. All three versions were based on "Utility" front ends, pioneered by the Ford-Ferguson.

The utility front gave a tractor a lower center of gravity and a higher roll center. These were features needed for stability with mounted implements. The downward-extended kingpins allowed reasonable crop clearance not possible with straight standard-tread front axles.

The three versions were the LU (Low Utility) with 17 inches of front axle clearance, the HU (High Utility) with 24 inches and the RU (Row crop Utility) with 20 inches. An Orchard version was available, but was in reality, a LU with orchard options (fenders and lowered steering wheel).

While the old 1010 had been essentially a Model 430 with a four-cylinder engine replacing the two-cylinder unit, the new 1020 was a clean-sheet-of-paper design. Waterloo engineers had primary responsibility, but with inputs from Dubuque and Mannheim engineering. The gasoline and diesel engines selected had three cylinders. The diesel used direct injection of the fuel into the combustion chamber, a scheme that negated the use of glow plugs. Since inline three-cylinder engines, like sixes, are naturally balanced, the need for a balance shaft was eliminated.

An eight-speed transmission was provided. In 1967, a power shift auxiliary with amplified torque was offered. Alternatively, a shuttle shift similar to that offered on the Model 440C and others was available. This latter was ideal for loader work.

Other big-tractor features found on the compact 1020 included a front-mounted fuel tank, "wet" hydraulic power brakes and a hydraulic system for a three-point hitch. Also there were two remote circuits, planetary final drives to the rear wheels, and the optional dual 540/1000 rpm PTO, rear and/or mid-ships.

Options included an adjustable-tread swept-back front axle in place of a straight adjustable axle. Various tire options were available plus a differential lock, power steering, deluxe seat, rack and pinion rear wheel adjusters, power adjustable rear wheels, foot throttle, Roll-Gard ROPS, and even a belt pulley.

Model 1020
Data and Specifications

Overall Years Built: 1965-1973
Built at: Dubuque, Iowa

Available configurations:
   row crop utility (RU)
   low utility (LU)
   high crop utility (HU)
   (Orchard/ grove tractors were LU models with orchard options.)

Wheels/Tires
Model 1020RU
   Front: 5.00-16 standard—6.00-16, 7.50-15, 9.00-10 optional
   Rear: 11.2-28 standard—12.4-28, 13.6-28, 14.9-28, 16.9-24, 18.4-16 optional

Wheels/Tires cont.
Model 1020HU
   Front: 5.50-16 standard—6.00-16, 7.50-15, 9.00-10 optional
   Rear: 12.4-36 standard—13.9-36 optional

Model 1020LU
   Front: 5.00-15 standard—6.00-16, 7.50-16, 9.00-10 optional
   Rear: 11.2-24 standard—no options offered

Engine Options:
   Vertical 3-cylinder, overhead valves, four-cycle

Gasoline

- Number of Cylinders: 3
- Bore & Stroke: 3.86 x 3.86 inches
- Displacement: 135.5 cid
- Rated RPM: 2500
- Cooling: Pump
- Compression Ratio: 7.5:1

Diesel

- Number of Cylinders: 3
- Bore & Stroke: 3.86 x 4.33 inches
- Displacement: 152.0 cid
- Rated RPM: 2500
- Cooling: Pump
- Compression Ratio: 16.3:1

Transmission:

Gear	Speed (mph)	
	Low	High
1	1.1	1.5
2	1.6	2.1
3	2.3	3.1
4	3.2	4.3
5	4.3	5.8
6	6.1	8.2
7	9.1	12.2
8	12.7	17.1
R-1	1.3	1.7
R-2	1.8	2.4
R-3	2.7	3.6
R-4	3.8	5.1

Shipping weight:
   Gasoline 4,210 lbs.
   Diesel   4,260 lbs.

Length: 120 inches

Width: 61 inches

Height: 51 inches (to top of hood)

Wheelbase: 81 inches (straight axle)

Price, new: RU Diesel—$4,500

Nebraska Test Data
Model 1020U Gas
Test Number 935
Date: 5-1966
Max. belt. hp.: 38.82
Max. available drawbar hp.*: 31.64
Specific fuel consumption hp.-hrs./gal.: 10.49
Weight as tested (lbs.): 5,940

Model 1020U Diesel
Test Number 937
Date: 5-1966
Max. belt. hp.: 38.92
Max. available drawbar hp.*: 31.81
Specific fuel consumption hp.-hrs./gal.: 14.76
Weight as tested (lbs.): 5,944

Serial Numbers Vs. Year Model*

Year	Beginning Serial Number
1965	14501
1966	14682
1967	42715
1968	65184
1969	82409
1970	102039
1971	117500
1972	134700
1973	157109

*Credible sources question these serial number breaks, but they line up with Deere publications.

The larger of the two Dubuque New Generation tractors, the Model 2010 filled the 45 to 50 horsepower niche, and had about 10 hp more than its smaller sibling, the Model 1010. Although there was no correlation between the Thirty Series and the New Generation tractors, the 2010 roughly replaced the 630.

When unveiled at Deere Days in Dallas on Aug. 30, 1960, the 2010 was there with four versions. (The crawler would come later.) All had eight-speed Synchro-Range transmissions. Gasoline and LPG versions used a 145-cid engine, while the new diesel boasted 165 cid.

The new diesel was of the "glow-plug start" type with a 19:1 compression ratio, unlike its Waterloo cousins, which used direct-injection diesels. Gone was the pony-motor starter. All the New Generation diesels had only the electric cranking option.

The row-crop version of the 2010 was available with a Roll-O-Matic narrow front, single front wheel, or with an adjustable wide front of either 50 to 74 inches, or 62 to 88 inches. Manual or power adjustable rear wheels were an option on all the versions except the crawler.

For the row crop utility tractors, either straight or swept-back adjustable front axles were available in the same two adjusting ranges as the row-crop version. The Special row crop utility model, which came out in 1963, was a stripped-down, lower-cost version with a pan seat. It was available only with a diesel engine. Most were exported south of the border.

High crop tractors offered the same options except the wide front axle adjustment range was 54 to 84 inches. Tire sizes were also different for the high crop version.

The agricultural crawler version of the Model 2010 came out in February 1963. It was essentially the same as the Industrial crawler, except for green paint. The shuttle-shift was not available on the ag version. The 1963 model year also saw a round of improvements to the 2010, especially to the diesel engine to overcome problems that had arisen. The engine, with its glow-plug starting system, had always been a hard starter and had never been completely satisfactory.

The crawler versions of the 2010 were canceled in late 1964, as the Industrial side of John Deere had become a separate division and was coming out with its own line of tractors.

Model 2010
Data and Specifications

Overall Years Built: 1961-1965
Built at: Dubuque, Iowa
Available configurations:

Code	Production
row crop (R)	BE
row crop utility (RU)	BD
special row crop utility (RUS)	BK
high crop (H)	BF
ag crawler (CA)	BA

Engine code:
1 = gasoline
2 = LPG
3 = diesel

Wheels/Tires:
row crop (R)
    Front: 6.00-14/6.50-16 /9.00-10
    Rear: 11.2/12.4/13.9-36
row crop utility (RU)
    Front: 6.00/6.50/7.50-16
    Rear: 12.4/13.6/14.9-28   16.9-26
special row crop utility (RUS)
    Front: 6.00/6.50/7.50-16
    Rear: 12.4/13.6/14.9-28   16.9-26
high crop (H)
    Front: 6.00/6.50/7.50-16
    Rear: 11.2/12.4/13.6-38

Engine options:
Gasoline/LPG
    Number of Cylinders: 4
    Bore & Stroke: 3.625 x 3.5 inches
    Displacement: 144.5 cid
    Rated RPM: 2500
    Cooling: Pump
Diesel
    Number of Cylinders: 4
    Bore & Stroke: 3.875 x 3.5 inches
    Displacement: 165 cid
    Rated RPM: 2500
    Cooling: Pump
Transmission: Synchro-Range, eight-speed
Travel speeds from 2.67 mph to 19.3 mph (RU) and
    from 1.48 mph to 6.69 mph (CA).

Optional Equipment: (partial list)
    Three-point hitch, with or without Quick-
        Coupler.
    Power steering.
    Single or dual hydraulics.
    Live 540/1000 rpm PTO.
    Deluxe seat.

Basic Weight:
    Wheel tractor:
    5,054 lbs. (RU1)
    5,120 lbs. (RU3)
    9,550 lbs. (CA1)
    9,645 lbs. (CA3)

Price, new:
Wheel tractors: $4,130-$4,350
Crawler: $5,866-$5,950
Diesel option: $ 800

Nebraska Test Data
Model 2010RU Gas
Test Number 800
Date: 6-1961
Max. belt. hp.: 46.86
Max. available drawbar hp.*: 39.12
Specific fuel consumption hp.-hrs./gal.: 11.79
Weight as tested (lbs.): 6,310

Model 2010RU Diesel
Test Number 799
Date: 6-1961
Max. belt. hp.: 46.67
Max. available drawbar hp.*: 39.28
Specific fuel consumption hp.-hrs./gal.: 12.78
Weight as tested (lbs.): 6,392

Model 2010CA Gas
Test Number 829
Date: 10-1962
Max. belt. hp.: 47.45
Max. available drawbar hp.*: 38.86
Specific fuel consumption hp.-hrs./gal.: 11.74
Weight as tested (lbs.): 9,550

Model 2010CA Diesel
Test Number 830
Date: 10-1962
Max. belt. hp.: 47.72
Max. available drawbar hp.*: 38.08
Specific fuel consumption hp.-hrs./gal.: 14.11
Weight as tested (lbs.): 9,645

*At the beginning of the 1959 testing season, changes were made in the way drawbar power was assessed. Rather than maximum low-gear drawbar pull, maximum available drawbar horsepower was recorded. This was based on a combination of pull and speed. For the crawlers, maximum low gear pull was recorded. Also at the beginning of 1959, belt power testing was discontinued in favor of PTO testing.

Model Variations: First and Last Serial Numbers and Build Dates

Model	First/last	Serial number	Build date
Crawler Gas/LPG	None		
Crawler Diesel	First	34341	2-11-63
	Last	58838	11-16-64
Row Crop Utility-LPG	First	15885	4-18-61
	Last	67000	8-20-65
Row Crop Utility-Gas	First	10001	6-1-60
	Last	68160	9-28-65
Row Crop Utility-Diesel	First	10138	8-3-60
	Last	68122	9-27-65
Spec. Row Crop Utility	First	26404	6-5-62
	Last	68193	9-29-65
Row Crop Gas	First	10108	7-26-60
	Last	68259	9-29-65
Row Crop LPG	First	13550	2-22-61
	Last	68171	9-28-65
Row Crop Diesel	First	10126	8-1-60
	Last	68252	9-29-65
High Crop LPG	First	17644	6-7-61
	Last	54415	7-10-64
High Crop Gas	First	10016	6-29-60
	Last	68079	9-24-65
High Crop Diesel	First	15705	4-13-61
	Last	68140	9-27-65

Model 2010 Serial Number vs. Year Model

Year	Beginning Serial Number
1966	10001
1967	19240*
1968	29001**
1969	42001
1970	54826

Last Serial Number – 68259

*   27880-29000 Not Used

** 40264-42000 Not Used

Model 2020

The Model 2020, which replaced the 2010 in 1965, was the product of World-Wide Tractor thinking that had been going on at Deere since the introduction of the New Generation line. Catering to European desires, the new 2020 would be offered only in the "Utility"configuration, since tricycle row-crops found homes only in the US. The Utility configuration, pioneered by Henry Ford and Harry Ferguson, would have three variations to satisfy worldwide tastes.

There would be a Row-crop Utility (RU), a Hi-crop Utility (HU) and a Low Utility (LU). While no narrow fronts would be available, the RU and the LU would offer adjustable swept front axles with good crop clearance. The LU was excellent for loader work and was available with additional low-profile features and orchard fenders for grove operations.

New gasoline and direct-injection diesel engines were made for the 2020. These four-cylinder engines featured counter-rotating balancers for extremely smooth running. A collar-shift eight-speed transmission was offered, but a two-speed auxiliary was an option. It functioned much like Harvester's Torque Amplifier. A shuttle-shift option was desirable for loader work, but could not be combined with the auxiliary. Power steering was standard equipment and much needed when using a heavy front-end loader.

Record keeping at the Dubuque factory was much less exact than at Waterloo, so the numbers of each type of 2020 are not available. In fact, the serial number versus year built data is questionable. The best available is presented in the Data section.

One of the rarest of the later John Deere tractors, this 1967 Grove is one of 21 built.
Owner: Keller Collection

Model 2020
Data and Specifications

Overall Model Years Built: 1965-1971

Built at: Dubuque, Iowa
Available configurations:
   RU (Row crop Utility)
   LU (Low Utility)
   HU (Hi-Crop Utility)

Wheels/Tires
Model RU
   Front: 6.00-16/7.50-15/7.50-16/9.00-10
   Rear: 12.4/13.6/14.9/16.9-28
      16.9-24/16.9/18.4-26
Model LU
   Front: 6.00-15/9.00-10/7.50-16
   Rear: 12.2/14.9/16.9-24
Model HU
   Front: 6.00-16/7.50-15/7.50-16/7.50-18
   Rear: 12.4/13.9/14.9-36
      13.6/15.5-38

Engine Options:
Engine code:
   1 = gasoline
   3 = diesel

Gasoline
   Number of cylinders: 4
   Bore & stroke: 3.86 x 3.86 inches
   Displacement: 180.7 cid
   Rated RPM: 2500
   Cooling: Pump/therm.
   Compression Ratio: 7.5:1

Diesel
   Number of cylinders: 4
   Bore & stroke: 3.86 x 4.31 inches
   Displacement: 201.8 cid
   Rated RPM: 2500
   Cooling: Pump/therm.
   Compression Ratio: 16.3:1

Transmission: 8 speed constant mesh, collar shift and 4 reverse speeds.
   0.7 to 17 mph with 14.9-28 tires

Height: 61 inches (to top of hood)
Wheelbase: 85.75 inches (straight front axle)
Weight: 5,500 lbs (shipping, gasoline engine; add 80 lbs. for diesel)

Standard Equipment: (partial list)
   Gasoline engine
   Hydraulic system (single)
   Rear rockshaft with three-point hitch
      (Category 2)
   540 rpm PTO (live)
   Adjustable swept-back front axle (RU and LU)
   Adjustable straight front axle (HU)
   Power steering
   Fenders with lights
   Drawbar
   Cushion seat
   Tach/hour meter
   Fuel gauge
   Alternator, 12V

Optional Equipment: (partial list)
   Diesel engine
   Hydraulic 2-speed auxiliary gearbox
   Shuttle shift transmission
   540 /1000 PTO
   Midships PTO
   Deluxe seat
   Power adjust wheels
   Foot throttle
   Remote hydraulics
   Roll-Gard ROPS
   Low-profile equipment and orchard fenders
      (LU)

Price, new:
$5,788 (Row-crop diesel)

Model 2020 Serial Number vs. Year Model	
Year	Beginning Serial Number
1965	14502
1966	14680
1967	42721
1968	65176
1969	82404
1970	102032
1971	117500

Nebraska Test Data

Model 2020 Gas
Test Number 936
Date: 5-1966
Max. belt. hp.: 53.91
Max. available drawbar hp.*: 43.94
Specific fuel consumption hp.-hrs./gal.: 11.17
Weight as tested (lbs.): 7,435

Model 2020 Diesel
Test Number 938
Date: 5-1966
Max. belt. hp.: 54.09
Max. available drawbar hp.*: 45.9
Specific fuel consumption hp.-hrs./gal.: 15.33
Weight as tested (lbs.): 7,310

Grove tractors can be distinguished by their hand-clutch (the tall lever on the left). This one has a gasoline engine and a collar-shift transmission.
Owner: Keller Collection

None of the Dubuque, or Mannheim-built tractors were offered in the tricycle front configuration by 1966, and the smallest of the Waterloo tractors (available as a tricycle) was the 65 hp Model 3020. Deere's marketing people realized sales opportunities were being missed for a smaller tricycle-front in the 45 to 55 hp range. The 2020 model from Dubuque could not accommodate a tricycle front without expensive modification, nor would "turning-down" 3020 be any less expensive to build than the 65 hp version. In a real stroke of synergism, it was decided to put a 2020 engine in a 3020 (modified) chassis. Economies of scale would bring costs down for both models, and the Model 2510 would fit right in between its two benefactors.

Waterloo engineers had designed the new 2020 engines, so fitting them to the 3020 chassis and transmissions presented no problems. The Model 2510 was aimed directly at the smaller American row-crop farmer, so only row-crop and Hi-Crop versions were offered, and only with gasoline or diesel engines. The two transmission choices were the Synchro-Range, or the Power Shift, both eight-speed units.

Only in America, it seemed, was there a demand for tricycle front tractors. Especially the corn growers liked them for both cultivating and for use with mounted pickers. This interest in tricycle fronts would soon wane in America, as well however, as chemical weed control and dedicated harvesters became the norm. The 2510 filled the niche in the meantime.

The John Deere 2510 came out in 1965. It was the last of the "New Generation Tractors" and was positioned between the 3010 and the 2010. This is a 1966 diesel version.
Owner: Marv Mathiowetz, Princeton, Minnesota

Overall model years built: 1966-1968
Built at: Waterloo, Iowa
Available configurations:
Row crop
Hi-Crop

Front End Options:
Dual tricycle, Dual tricycle with Roll-O-Matic (regular or heavy-duty), single front wheel, adjustable wide front (narrow, 40 to 80 inch tread, or wide, 56 to 88 inch tread)

Wheels/Tires:
Row crop
Front: 6.00-14/7.50-15/6.00-16
Rear: 12.4/13.6/15.5-38
Standard
SFW: 7.50-16/9.00-10
Hi-Crop
Front: 7.50-18/7.50-20
Rear: 13.6-38/15.5-38

Engine Options:
Engine code:
1 = gasoline
3 = diesel

Gasoline
Number of cylinders: 4
Bore & Stroke: 3.86 x 3.86 inches
Displacement: 180.4 cid
Rated RPM: 2500
Cooling: Pump

Diesel
Number of cylinders: 4
Bore & Stroke: 3.86 x 4.33 inches
Displacement: 202.7 cid
Rated RPM: 2500
Cooling: Pump

Transmission:
Synchro-Range, eight speeds
Travel speeds from 1.78 to 15.76 mph
Power Shift, eight speeds forward, four reverse
Travel speeds from 1.67 to 17.49 mph

Standard Equipment:
Gasoline engine
Synchro-Range transmission
Dual tricycle front end
Power steering
Power brakes
Fenders with lights
Drawbar
Deluxe seat

Optional Equipment: (partial list)
Diesel engine
Power Shift transmission
Hi-crop equipment
Front-end options
Rear rockshaft
Three-point hitch
Single or dual hydraulics
Live 540/1000 rpm PTO (rear)
Front PTO (1000 rpm)
Power differential lock
Long and extra-long rear axles

Basic Weight:
Row-crop (gasoline) Power Shift: .6,575 lbs.
Row-crop (gasoline) Synchro-Range: 6,245 lbs.
Row-crop (diesel) Power Shift: 6,745 lbs.
Row-crop (diesel) Synchro-Range: 6,525 lbs.

Price, New:
Row-crop – gasoline $3,975 (1966)
Diesel option $ 500
Hi-crop option $1,200
Power Shift option $ 600

Nebraska Test Data

Model 2510 Gas, Power Shift
Test Number 913
Date: 9-1965
Max. belt. hp.: 49.57
Max. available drawbar hp.: 42.44
Specific fuel consumption hp.-hrs./gal.: 10.27
Weight as tested (lbs.): 8,045

Model 2510 Gas, Synchro-Range
Test Number 914
Date: 9-1965
Max. belt. hp.: 53.74
Max. available drawbar hp.: 45.21
Specific fuel consumption hp.-hrs./gal.: 11.28
Weight as tested (lbs.): 7,715

Model 2510 Diesel, Power Shift
Test Number 915
Date: 10-1965
Max. belt. hp.: 50.66
Max. available drawbar hp.: 43.54
Specific fuel consumption hp.-hrs./gal.: 14.22
Weight as tested (lbs.): 8,215

Model 2510 Diesel, Synchro
Test Number 916
Date: 10-1965
Max. belt. hp.: 54.96
Max. available drawbar hp.: 46.82
Specific fuel consumption hp.-hrs./gal.: 15.84
Weight as tested (lbs.): 8,485

Model 2510 Serial Number vs. Year Model

Year	Beginning Serial Number
1966	1001
1967	8958
1968	14291
Last Serial Number – 16501	

The 2510 had a Dubuque-built 2010 engine in a Waterloo-built 3010 frame. It was a nominally 55 hp tractor that fit between the 3020 and the 2020 models. Gasoline or diesel engines and Synchro-Range or Power Shift transmissions were options.

The John Deere Model 2520 was one of the greatest tractors of all times. Sometimes called "the poor-man's 4020," the 2520 had all the features, but at a smaller size and price. Further, the very-few deficiencies found in three years of producing its forerunner, the 2510, were corrected in the 2520.

For the 1969 model year, John Deere Waterloo tractors were given more power. The 2520 was upgraded from around 50 to around 60 hp. The next in the lineup was the 3020, up from 65 hp to a little over 70. For the 2520 to gain this power increase, the gasoline engine was given the bore and stroke of the diesel engine used in the 2510. The new 2520 diesel got a bore increase of

0.16 inches while the stroke remained the same as on the 2510.

A major improvement given the 2520 was the relocation of the hydraulic controls from the left side of the dash to the right side of the seat. This location had become more-or-less standard for the industry, and seemed a much more natural position.

Another significant innovation for the 2520 was the optional ROPS (Roll-Over Protection System), available both with, or without a factory cab. The fact that the ROPS was an option seems hard to believe today, but it was well into the '70s before these became commonplace.

The John Deere 2510 was considered one of the best tractors ever made, yet Deere improved upon it with the Model 2520. The most notable improvement was increased engine displacement, putting the tractor over 60 hp and improving its lugging ability.
Owner: Keller Collection

Years built: 1969-1972
Built at: Waterloo, Iowa
Available configurations:
- Row crop
- Hi-Crop

Front End Options:
Dual tricycle, Dual tricycle with Roll-O-Matic (regular or heavy-duty), single front wheel, adjustable wide front (narrow – 40 to 80 inch tread, or wide – 56 to 88 inch tread).

Wheels/Tires:
Row crop
- Front: 6.00-14/7.50-15/6.00-16
- Rear: 12.4/13.6/15.5-38
- SFW: 7.50-16/9.00-10

Hi-Crop
- Front: 7.50-18/7.50-20
- Rear: 13.6-38/15.5-38

Engine Options:
Engine code:
- 1 = gasoline
- 3 = diesel

Gasoline
- Number of Cylinders: 4
- Bore & Stroke: 3.86 x 4.33 inches
- Displacement: 202.7 cid
- Rated RPM: 2500
- Cooling: Pump

Diesel
- Number of Cylinders: 4
- Bore & Stroke: 4.02 x 4.33 inches
- Displacement: 219.8 cid
- Rated RPM: 2500
- Cooling: Pump

Transmission:
Synchro-Range, eight speeds
Travel speeds from 1.78 to 15.76 mph
Power Shift, eight speeds forward, four reverse
Travel speeds from 1.67 to 17.49 mph

Standard Equipment: (partial list)
- Gasoline engine
- Synchro-Range transmission
- Hydraulic system (single)
- Rear rockshaft with three-point hitch
- 540/1000 rpm PTO
- Adjustable wide front end
- Power steering
- Power brakes
- Fenders with lights
- Drawbar
- Deluxe seat
- Tach/hour meter
- Fuel gauge
- Foot throttle

Optional Equipment: (partial list)
- Diesel engine
- Power Shift transmission
- Hi-crop equipment
- Front-end options
- Dual or triple remote hydraulics
- Live 1000 rpm PTO (rear and mid-ship)
- Front PTO (1000 rpm)
- Power differential lock
- Long and extra-long rear axles
- Horn
- Roll-Gard ROPS, with/without canopy*
- Roll-Gard cab*
- *Not available on Hi-Crop versions

Basic Weight:
Row-crop (gasoline) Power Shift: 7,390 lbs.
Row-crop (gasoline) Synchro-Range: 7,130 lbs.
Row-crop (diesel) Power Shift: 7,425 lbs.
Row-crop (diesel) Synchro-Range: 7,180 lbs.

Price, New:

Row-crop – gasoline	$5,166 (1969)
Diesel option	$650
Hi-crop option	$1,550
Power Shift option	$780

Nebraska Test Data

Model 2520 Gas, Power Shift
Test Number 1002
Date: 3-1969
Max. belt. hp.: 56.98
Max. available drawbar hp.: 48.09
Specific fuel consumption hp.-hrs./gal.: 10.3
Weight as tested (lbs.): 8,990

Model 2520 Gas, Synchro-Range
Test Number 1003
Date: 3-1969
Max. belt. hp.: 60.16
Max. available drawbar hp.: 54.45
Specific fuel consumption hp.-hrs./gal.: 10.46
Weight as tested (lbs.): 8,955

Model 2520 Diesel, Power Shift
Test Number 993
Date: 10-1968
Max. belt. hp.: 56.28
Max. available drawbar hp.: 45.98
Specific fuel consumption hp.-hrs./gal.: 14.68
Weight as tested (lbs.): 9,040

Model 2520 Diesel, Synchro
Test Number 992
Date: 10-1968
Max. belt. hp.: 61.29
Max. available drawbar hp.: 55.86
Specific fuel consumption hp.-hrs./gal.: 15.27
Weight as tested (lbs.): 8,955

Model 2520 Serial Number vs. Year Model

Year	Beginning Serial Number
1969	017000
1970	019416
1971	022000
1972	022915

Last Serial Number – 023865 (not all intervening numbers used)

Shown is a 1969 Model 2520 with a 202 cid gasoline engine. The diesel was now 219 cid. This is one of only eight gasoline Hi-Crops made. It has the Synchro-Range transmission and 15.5-38 rear tires.
Owner: Keller Collection

Model 3010

The John Deere Model 3010 was the smaller of the two Waterloo-built New Generation tractors announced during Deere Days in Dallas in August 1960. It was essentially a scaled down, four-cylinder version of the six-cylinder Model 4010.

The 3010 featured the same closed-center hydraulic system with three circuits and a variable-displacement pump. One circuit was for power steering, one for power brakes, and one for the rockshaft/three-point hitch and remote implements.

The engines used in the 3020 were offered in gasoline, LPG and diesel versions. They had the same bore and stroke as the 4020 engines, but with two fewer cylinders. The LPG version of the 3010 had the distinction of being the only Deere tractors to have their fuel tanks fully concealed under the hood. The transmission was the new Synchro-Range eight speed unit with two reverse speeds.

Model 3010 production included some industrial versions and some foreign variations. An orchard version was available in 1962, but was not offered with the LPG engine. It was based on the Row crop Utility configuration. No Hi-Crop 3010s were shown in the catalog, but it is suspected that some were made, either as custom factory jobs, or as dealer conversions.

Shown is a 1960 gasoline 3010 Row-Crop Utility with optional adjustable-tread axles.
Owner: Keller Collection

The Synchro-Range shift, power steering and speed-hour meter were standard. For options, it has a narrow front with Roll-O-Matic, three-point hitch, deluxe seat, 14.9-38 rear tires, and PTO.

Overall years built: 1961-1963

Built at: Waterloo, Iowa

Available configurations :

Row crop

Utility

Standard Tread

Orchard

Axle Options:

Row crop, front: Dual tricycle, Regular Roll-O-Matic, Heavy-duty Roll-O-Matic, Single front wheel, Adjustable wide-front, 48-80 inches

Row crop, rear: Regular-length adjustable, 57 to 88 inches; Long, 62 to 98 inches (58-104 inches with offset wheels)

Standard Tread, front: Fixed length, 55 inches, and adjustable length, 52 to 66 inches.

Standard Tread, rear: Adjustable, 52 to 79 inches.

Row crop Utility, front: Fixed length, 55.5 or 61 inches and adjustable length, 50 to 79 inches.

Row crop Utility, rear: Regular length, 60 or 80 inches and adjustable, 50 to 79 inches.

Wheels/Tires:

Row Crop Tractors:

Front: 6.00-14, 6.00-16, 7.50-15

SFW: 9.00-10, 6.50-16 (36" rears); 7.50-16, 11.00-12 (38" rears)

Rear: 13.9-36, 13.6, 14.9, or 15.5-38

Standard Tread Tractors:

Front: 6.50-16, 7.50-16, 7.50-18

Rear: 16.9-30, 18.4-30, and 18.4-34

Row crop Utility and Orchard Tractors:

Front: 6.50-16, 7.50-16

Rear: 13.6-28, 14.9-28

Wheelbase: 90.0 inches, Row crop

81.5 inches, Row crop Utility

92.75 inches, Row crop Utility

(Optional long WB)

Engine Options:

Gasoline

Number of Cylinders: 4

Bore & Stroke: 4.0 x 4.0 in.

Displacement: 201 cid

Rated RPM: 2200

Cooling: Pump

Compression Ratio: 7.5:1

LPG

Number of Cylinders: 4

Bore & Stroke: 4.0 x 4.0 in.

Displacement: 201 cid

Rated RPM: 2200

Cooling: Pump

Compression Ratio: 9.0:1

Diesel

Number of Cylinders: 4

Bore & Stroke: 4.125 x 4.75 in.

Displacement: 254 cid

Rated RPM: 2200

Cooling: Pump

Compression Ratio: 16.4:1

Transmission:

Synchro-Range, eight-speed, two in reverse
Travel speeds from 1.7 mph to 14.50 mph

3010 Tractors, Weight and Price

Gasoline Tractors:
Row Crop
    Shipping Weight, lbs.: 5,314
    Price, New (1961): $3,525
Standard
    Shipping Weight, lbs.: 5,805
    Price, New (1961): $3,792
Row Crop Utility
    Shipping Weight, lbs.: 5,372
    Price, New (1961): $3,631

LPG Tractors:
Row Crop
    Shipping Weight, lbs.: 5,433
    Price, New (1961) $3,800
Standard
    Shipping Weight, lbs.: 5,924
    Price, New (1961): $4,067
Row Crop Utility
    Shipping Weight, lbs.: 5,491
    Price, New (1961): $3,906

Diesel Tractors:
Row Crop
    Shipping Weight, lbs.: 5,606
    Price, New (1961): $4,100
Standard
    Shipping Weight, lbs.: 6,000
    Price, New (1961): $4,367
Row Crop Utility
    Shipping Weight, lbs.: 5,568
    Price, New (1961): $4,206

Nebraska Test Data

Model 3010 Diesel
Test Number 762
Date: 9-1960
Max. belt. hp.: 59.44
Max. available drawbar hp.: 52.77
Specific fuel consumption hp.-hrs./gal.: 14.52
Weight as tested (lbs.): 8,640

Model 3010 Gas
Test Number 763
Date: 9-1960
Max. belt. hp.: 55.09
Max. available drawbar hp.: 50.98
Specific fuel consumption hp.-hrs./gal.: 10.7
Weight as tested (lbs.): 8,470

Model 3010 LPG
Test Number 764
Date: 9-1960
Max. belt. hp.: 55.39
Max. available drawbar hp.: 49.22
Specific fuel consumption hp.-hrs./gal.: 8.46
Weight as tested (lbs.): 8,535

Model 3010 Serial Number vs. Year Model

Year	Beginning Serial Number
1961	1000
1962	10801
1963	32400

Last Serial Number – 46952

This Model 3010 has the diesel engine option. More than half of all 3010s had diesel engines.
Owner: Keller Collection

Model 3020

The John Deere Model 3020 was much the same as the 3010 it replaced in 1964, but it had a bit more power, a traction lock, the optional Power Shift transmission and the optional FWA (Front Wheel Assist) made available in 1968.

International Harvester's Model 706 (and 756, which came out in 1966) was providing stiff competition for the 3020. This was especially true after I-H replaced the "glow-plug" diesel with a larger displacement German-built direct injection diesel. The Harvester tractors offered smooth six-cylinder power to compete with Deere's four. In 1969, Deere gave the 3020 a substantial displacement increase for the gasoline and LPG (Liquefied Petroleum Gas) engines. The 3020's diesel was holding its own, and remained the same displacement, but with internal improvements.

A general upgrade in 1969, in areas besides the engine, kept the 3020 on the cutting edge. The new console on the right side of the driver was a great improvement in ergonomics. Also new in 1969 was a 12-volt negative ground electrical system, powered by an alternator.

This 1967 John Deere 3020 narrow-front row-crop had only 1100 hours when the photo was taken. It has a gasoline engine, three-point hitch, deluxe seat and power steering. Owner: Arvin Busenitz, Newton, Kansas

This gasoline Hi-Crop 3020 has the optional Power-Shift. It is a 1972 model with the 241-cid engine.
Owner: Keller Collection

Overall years built: 1964-1972

Built at: Waterloo, Iowa

Available configurations:

Row crop

Row crop Utility

Standard Tread

Orchard

Hi-Crop

Axle Options:

Row crop, front: Dual tricycle, Regular Roll-O-Matic, Heavy-duty Roll-O-Matic, Single front wheel and adjustable wide-front, 48 to 80 inches.

Row crop, rear: Regular-length adjustable, 57 to 88 inches. Long, 62 to 98 inches (58 to 104 inches with offset wheels).

Standard Tread, front: Fixed length, 55 inches and adjustable length, 52 to 66 inches.

Standard Tread, rear: Adjustable, 52 to 79 inches.

Row crop Utility, front: Fixed length, 55.5 or 61 inches and adjustable length, 50 to 79 inches.

Row crop Utility, rear: Regular length, 60 or 80 inches and adjustable, 50 to 79 inches.

Wheels/Tires:

Row Crop Tractors

Front: 6.00-14, 6.00-16, 7.50-15

SFW: 9.00-10, 6.50-16 (36" rears); 7.50-16, 11.00-12 (38" rears)

Rear: 13.9-36, 13.6, 14.9, or 15.5-38

Standard Tread Tractors

Front: 6.50-16, 7.50-16, 7.50-18

Rear: 16.9-30, 18.4-30, and 18.4-34

Row crop Utility and Orchard Tractors

Front: 6.50-16, 7.50-16

Rear: 13.6-28, 14.9-28

Hi-Crop Tractors

Front: 7.50-18

Rear: 15.5-38

Wheelbase:

90.0 inches, Row crop

81.5 inches, Row crop Utility

92.75 inches, Row crop Utility (Optional long WB)

92.8 inches, Hi-Crop

Engine Options:

Gasoline

Number of cylinders: 4

Bore & Stroke (Early) 4.25 x 4.0 in.

Displacement: 227 cid

Bore & Stroke (after 1969) 4.25 x 4.25 in.

Displacement: 241 cid

Rated RPM: 2500

Cooling: Pump

Compression Ratio: 7.5:1

LPG

Number of cylinders: 4

Bore & Stroke (Early) 4.25 x 4.0 in.

Displacement: 227 cid

Bore & Stroke (after 1969) 4.25 x 4.25 in.

Displacement: 241 cid

Rated RPM: 2500

Cooling: Pump

Compression Ratio: 9.01:1

Diesel

Number of cylinders: 4

Bore & Stroke (Early) 4.25 x 4.75 in.

Displacement: 270 cid

Bore & Stroke (after 1969) 4.25 x 4.75 in.

Displacement: 270 cid

Rated RPM: 2500

Cooling: Pump

Compression Ratio: 16.5:1

Transmission:

Synchro-Range, eight-speed, two in reverse.

Synchro-Range Power Shift, eight-speeds, four in reverse.

Travel speeds from 1.9 mph to 19.50 mph (Power Shift).

2.0 mph to 17.6 mph (Synchro-Range).

3020 Tractors, Weight and Price

Gasoline Tractors

Row Crop

Basic weight, lbs: 7,395

Price, new (1967): $6,525

LPG

Row Crop

Basic weight, lbs: 7,545

Price, new (1967): $6,800

Diesel

Row Crop

Basic weight, lbs: 7,610

Price, new (1967): $7,100

Nebraska Test Data

Model 3020 Diesel
Test Number 848
Date: 10-1963
Engine disp. (cid)/tran: 270/PS
Max. belt. hp.: 65.28
Max. available drawbar hp.: 54.8
Specific fuel consumption hp.-hrs./gal.: 12.71
Weight as tested (lbs.): 9,585

Model 3020 Gas
Test Number 851
Date: 9-1963
Engine disp. (cid)/tran: 227/PS
Max. belt. hp.: 64.14
Max. available drawbar hp.: 54.6
Specific fuel consumption hp.-hrs./gal.: 10.37
Weight as tested (lbs.): 9,495

Model 3020 LPG
Test Number 852
Date: 10-1963
Engine disp. (cid)/tran: 227/PS
Max. belt. hp.: 64.7
Max. available drawbar hp.: 54.5
Specific fuel consumption hp.-hrs./gal.: 8.13
Weight as tested (lbs.): 9,605

Model 3020 Diesel
Test Number 940
Date: 5-1966
Engine disp. (cid)/tran: 270/SR
Max. belt. hp.: 71.26
Max. available drawbar hp.: 61.47
Specific fuel consumption hp.-hrs./gal.: 13.87
Weight as tested (lbs.): 9,915

Model 3020 Gas
Test Number 941
Date: 6-1966
Engine disp. (cid)/tran: 227/SR
Max. belt. hp.: 70.59
Max. available drawbar hp.: 61.38
Specific fuel consumption hp.-hrs./gal.: 10.66
Weight as tested (lbs.): 9,825

Model 3020 LPG
Test Number 942
Date: 6-1966
Engine disp. (cid)/tran: 227/SR
Max. belt. hp.: 70.7
Max. available drawbar hp.: 63.13
Specific fuel consumption hp.-hrs./gal.: 8.62
Weight as tested (lbs.): 9,836

Model 3020 Gas
Test Number 1010
Date: 6-1969
Engine disp. (cid)/tran: 241/PS
Max. belt. hp.: 67.13
Max. available drawbar hp.: 55.79
Specific fuel consumption hp.-hrs./gal.: 9.77
Weight as tested (lbs.): 10,320

Model 3020 Gas
Test Number 1011
Date: 5-1969
Engine disp. (cid)/tran: 241/SR
Max. belt. hp.: 71.37
Max. available drawbar hp.: 61.26
Specific fuel consumption hp.-hrs./gal.: 10.91
Weight as tested (lbs.): 10,220

Model 3020 Serial Number vs. Year Model

Year	Beginning Serial Number
1964	50000
1965	68000
1966	84000
1967	97266
1968	112933
1969	123000
1970	129897
1971	150000
1972	154197

The Model 3020 was similar to the 3010 it replaced in 1964, but it had more power, a traction lock and optional Power Shift transmission was available. There were gasoline, diesel and LPG versions. The Model 3020 was built from 1964 to 1972.
Owner: Arvin Busenitz, Newton, Kansas

The 3020 was offered from 1964 to 1972. The 3010 and 3020 tractors with LPG engines are rare, and difficult to spot, since their fuel tanks are not exposed like the rest.
Owner: Keller Collection

Model 4010

The largest and probably the most significant of the "New Generation" tractors introduced to dealers at the October 1960 Deere Days in Dallas was the mighty 4010. It was, at the time, the biggest John Deere. The farmer could now have his (or her) row crop tractor with more than 75 horsepower.

In typical Deere fashion, the 4010 could be obtained in a wide variety of configurations. Basically, it was available as a row crop, standard tread, high crop, or industrial. There was also a special export version of the standard. In row crops, there was the dual tricycle, the wide front, and the single front wheel arrangements. There were straight and heavy-duty versions of the single wheel and Roll-O-Matic dual tricycle front ends.

The 4010's major features were the new six-cylinder engine, the central hydraulic system, an 8-speed transmission, and the ergonomically designed platform and seat.

The new engine was an inline six. This configuration was arrived at after much experimentation with V-6, and V-4 cylinder arrangements. Experience had been gained with V-4s in the latest iteration of pony motors for the 30 Series diesels. In the larger sizes, smoothness was not their long suit, plus with 90 degrees between the cylinder banks, the engine was wider than desired. The V-6 arrangement required only 60 degrees between banks for balance. But as it turned out, the advantages of a V-type engine for a tractor were entirely subjective, adding to the cost and not to the value. Therefore, a straight six was chosen, despite criticisms of "me-too-ism" from those who thought Deere should maintain some element of the individualism they had enjoyed with the two-cylinder engine. The basic engine design accommodated the three fuels that would be used; gasoline, LPG and diesel, and it was designed for growth. Bore centers were the same, despite two different displacements of the spark ignition and diesel versions. The spark ignition versions used four main bearings, while the diesel version used seven.

This is the first Model 4010 made, Serial Number 1000. It is a diesel and has the narrow front end with Roll-O-Matic. Owner: Keller Collection

This Model 4010 has a three-point hitch and its rear tires are 16.9-38s.
Owner: Keller Collection

The new central hydraulic system design was a unique departure for tractors. For this approach, a page was taken from aircraft industry design standards. Rather than have the pump discharge excess flow through a pressure relief valve as had been done previously, a variable-displacement pump was used. When hydraulic power needs of this new system were satisfied, the pump went to near zero stroke, eliminating the heat generated and reducing parasitic engine power losses. The variable-displacement pump supplied pressure for raising implements, both three-point and remote, the power steering (there was no mechanical connection to the front wheels), power brakes, and the differential lock.

Power shift and torque converter transmissions were being exploited by Deere's competitors with some success, although problems persisted. One Mr. Harold Brock, who had been with Ford Motor Company from the days of the Model A car through the design of the famous N Series tractors, had a falling-out with Ford over their 10-speed power shift transmission (the Select-O-Speed).

Ford management insisted the transmission was ready for production and so introduced it in 1959 over the objections of Mr. Brock. Soon thereafter, Deere's relatively new chairman William Hewitt (who began his career in tractors with Ford), prevailed upon Harold Brock to join Deere. Mr. Brock's experience (and the subsequent problems Ford had with the original Select-O-Speeds) prompted Deere to stick with a selective gear, fixed-ratio transmission for the 4010, called the Synchro-Range.

Henry Dreyfuss and associates, the industrial design experts who had been involved in the design of Deere tractors since 1937, were commissioned to provide an optimum operator's station for the New Generation tractors. For the 4010, much research went into optimizing control placement and in providing a comfortable space. Dr. Janet Travell, an orthopedic specialist, along with the Dreyfuss team and Deere engineers, came up with a new seat that is still being copied 30 years later.

Overall years built: 1961-1963

Built at: Waterloo, Iowa

Available configurations:

Row crop (gasoline, LPG, diesel)

Standard (gasoline, LPG, diesel)

High crop (gasoline, LPG, diesel)

Special Std. (diesel, only)

Wheels/Tires:

Row Crop Tractors

Front: 6.00-16, 7.50-15

Rear: 13.6, 14.9, or 15.5-38; 16.9, or 18.4-34; 18-4-30

Power adjustable Rear Wheels: 34 or 38-inch wheels

High Crop Tractors

Front: 6.00-16, 7.50-15

Rear: 13.6, 14.9, or 15.5-38; 18.4-34

Standard Tread Tractors

Front: 6.00-16, 7.50-15

Rear: 18.4-30, 18.4-34, and 23.1-26

Wheelbase: 96 inches

Engine Options:

Gasoline

Number of Cylinders: 6

Bore & Stroke: 4.0 x 4.0 in.

Displacement: 302 cid

Rated RPM: 2200

Cooling: Pump

Compression Ratio: 7.5:1

LPG

Number of Cylinders: 6

Bore & Stroke: 4.0 x 4.0 in.

Displacement: 302 cid

Rated RPM: 2200

Cooling: Pump

Compression Ratio: 9.0:1

Diesel

Number of Cylinders: 6

Bore & Stroke: 4.125 x 4.75 in.

Displacement: 380 cid

Rated RPM: 2200

Cooling: Pump

Compression Ratio: 16.0:1

Transmission:

Synchro-Range, eight-speed

Travel speeds from 1.5 mph to 14.25 mph

Shipping weight: 7100 lbs. to 7500 lbs.

Price, new:

Gasoline Tractors	$4,116 to $5,285
Diesel option	$ 700
LPG option	$ 300
PTO	$ 177
3-point hitch	$ 179

Nebraska Test Data

Model 4010 Gas
Test Number 759
Date: 9-1960
Max. belt. hp.: 80.96
Max. available drawbar hp.*:
    71.25
Specific fuel consumption hp.-
    hrs./gal.: 11.26
Weight as tested (lbs.): 9,595

Model 4010 LPG
Test Number 760
Date: 9-1960
Max. belt. hp.: 80.60
Max. available drawbar hp.*:
    71.77
Specific fuel consumption hp.-
    hrs./gal.: 8.72
Weight as tested (lbs.): 9,735

Model 4010 Diesel
Test Number 761
Date: 9-1960
Max. belt. hp.: 84.0
Max. available drawbar hp.*:
    71.93
Specific fuel consumption hp.-
    hrs./gal.: 14.97
Weight as tested (lbs.): 9,775

*At the beginning of the 1959 testing season, changes were made in the way drawbar power was assessed. Rather than maximum low gear drawbar pull, maximum available drawbar horsepower was recorded. This was based on a combination of pull and speed. Also at the beginning of 1959, belt power testing was discontinued in favor of PTO testing

Shown is a Hi-Crop 4010 with and LPG fuel system. It is one of only 17 built. Owner: Keller Collection

Model 4010 Serial Number vs. Year Model

Year	Beginning Serial Number
1961	1000
1962	20201
1963	38200

Last Serial Number – 59313
Serial Numbers Scrapped – 390
Assigned to Monterey, Mexico - 350

Production Totals

Type	Fuel	Number Built
Row Crop	Gasoline	3,613
	LPG	4,459
	Diesel	36,736
Standard	Gasoline	98
	LPG	792
	Diesel	11,370
High Crop	Gasoline	*
	LPG	17
	Diesel	170
Industrial	Gasoline	10
	Diesel	170
Special Standard **	Diesel	36

*One built and shipped, but later returned and converted to diesel.

**Export only

The Model 4010 is powered by a six-cylinder engine that displaced 380 cid and produced 84 PTO horsepower.
Owner: Keller Collection

Any list of the most significant tractors of the 20th century should include the John Deere Model 4020. My own personal list, in order of their importance (in my estimation) is as follows:

John Deere 4020
Ford-Ferguson
Fordson
Farmall Regular
Caterpillar Diesel 60

Others would perhaps criticize these rankings, and would likely include some different makes, but I firmly believe the 4020 would at least stay in the top five on most lists. I like to think the ones I've selected had a lasting impact on tractors that followed by all makers.

Why is the 4020 so highly regarded? It was, as they say, almost without sin. The 4010 was a good tractor, but with the warts and blemishes removed, it became the 4020, the first tractor in history that was as nearly perfect as it could be made. Now, 40 years after it was first introduced, most of them are still at work. To buy one in decent shape today will cost you about twice as much as a new one did.

When the 4010 was designed as the flagship of the New Generation tractors, growth was built in to the critical components, so they could be easily upgraded as time went on. Despite the secrecy of the New Generation design project, International Harvester was remarkably well-informed, and soon came out with creditable competitors. Assuming their first look at the 4010 came in the fall of 1960, I-H did wonders to come out with their Model 806 in time for the 1963 model year. With it, they blew past the 4010 in horsepower.

Deere also was well informed about what I-H was doing and the 4020 trumped the 806 in power and in sophistication. The ergonomic engineering set industry standards.

The 4020 was built from 1964-1972. In 1969, general upgrades included optional front wheel assist (FWA). The 4020 also received a new console and a negative-ground 12-V electrical system with an alternator.
Owner: Keller Collection

The single-lever Power Shift transmission was a great convenience, although it did absorb a little more of the 4020's horsepower than did the Synchro-Range. Engineer Harold Brock (who was instrumental in the design of the Ford 9N, and those that followed) recounts that in 1959 he was fired from his job as chief engineer of the Ford Tractor Division because he refused to authorize production of tractors with Ford's new Select-O-Speed power shift transmission. He immediately went to work at Deere.

Ford encountered a disaster, which Deere avoided with Brock's help and with proper development. Ford eventually overcame their problems, but not without recalling tractors and getting a black-eye from their customers.

A general upgrade in 1969 kept the 4020 on the cutting edge. The new console on the right side of the driver overcame one of the few complaints – that the driver needed more than two hands when coming to the end of a row with multiple hook-ups behind. Also new in 1969 was the hydraulic FWA (Front Wheel Assist) and a 12-volt negative ground electrical system, powered by an alternator. Standard tractors were folded in with the Row Crops in 1969. Separate identifiers were eliminated.

The diesel version of the 4020 shown has the Roll-Gard ROPS with canopy, triple hydraulics, 18.4-34 rear tires and 11.2-24 front tires.
Owner: Keller Collection

Model 4020
Data and Specifications

Overall years built: 1964-1972
Built at: Waterloo, Iowa
Available configurations:

Row crop (gasoline, LPG, diesel)

Standard (gasoline, LPG, diesel)

High crop (gasoline, LPG, diesel)

Wheels/Tires:

Row Crop Tractors

Front: 6.00-16, 7.50-15, 7.5L-15

Rear: 13.6, 14.9, or 15.5-38; 16.9, or 18.4-34;
18-4-30

Power adjustable Rear Wheels: 34 or 38-inch
wheels

High Crop Tractors

Front: 6.00-16, 7.50-15, 7.5L-15

Rear: 13.6, 14.9, or 15.5-38; 18.4-34

Standard Tread Tractors

Front: 6.00-16, 7.50-15, 7.5L-15

Rear: 18.4-30, 18.4-34, and 23.1-26

Wheelbase: 98 inches (Row Crop)

Engine Options:
Gasoline

Number of Cylinders: 6

Bore & Stroke: (1963-65) 4.25 x 4.00 in.

Displacement: 340 cid

Bore & Stroke: (1966-72) 4.25 x 4.25 in.

Displacement: 362 cid

Rated RPM: 2200*

Cooling: Pump

Compression Ratio: 7.5:1

LPG

Number of Cylinders: 6

Bore & Stroke: (1963-65) 4.25 x 4.00 in.

Displacement: 340 cid

Bore & Stroke: (1966-72) 4.25 x 4.25 in.

Displacement: 362 cid

Rated RPM: 2200*

Cooling: Pump

Compression Ratio: 9.0:1

Diesel

Number of Cylinders: 6

Bore & Stroke: (1963-65) 4.25 x 4.75 in.

Displacement: 404 cid

Bore & Stroke: (1966-72) 4.25 x 4.75 in.

Displacement: 404 cid

Rated RPM: 2200*

Cooling: Pump

Compression Ratio: 16.5:1

*2500 rpm available with foot throttle for road
travel.

Transmission:

Synchro-Range, eight-speed.

Power Shift, eight speeds, straight-through no-
clutch shifting.

Travel speeds from 1.8 mph to 18.75 mph.

Shipping weight:

8100 lbs to 8600 lbs (Row Crop)

Clutch:

Synchro-Range, 12 in. dry disk, foot pedal
operated.

Power Shift, dry disk engine disconnect, hand
lever operated and "Inching Pedal."

Price, New:	1965	1969
Gasoline Tractors	$4,714	$7,750
	to $5,366	to $8,400
Options:		
Diesel Engine	$820	$890
LPG option	$335	$352
Standard Tread	$472	$300
Power Shift	$630	$710
3-point hitch	$195	included
PTO	$230	included
Remote Hydraulics	$150 (single),	single-
	$250 (dual)	included
		$145 dual
		$306 triple
Cab	$650	$1200
Roll-O-Matic	$70	N/A
Adj. Wide Front	$235	included

Nebraska Test Data

Model 4020 Diesel
Test Number 849
Date: 9-1963
Max. belt. hp.: 91.17
Max. available drawbar hp.: 76.36
Specific fuel consumption hp.-hrs./gal.: 14.2
Weight as tested (lbs.): 13,055
Engine disp./trans.: 404/SR

Model 4020 Gas
Test Number 850
Date: 9-1963
Max. belt. hp.: 88.09
Max. available drawbar hp.: 73.06
Specific fuel consumption hp.-hrs./gal.: 10.53
Weight as tested (lbs.): 13,135
Engine disp./trans.: 340/SR

Model 4020 LPG
Test Number 853
Date: 10-1963
Max. belt. hp.: 90.48
Max. available drawbar hp.: 75.19
Specific fuel consumption hp.-hrs./gal.: 8.95
Weight as tested (lbs.): 13,125
Engine disp./trans.: 340/SR

Model 4020 Diesel
Test Number 930
Date: 11-1965
Max. belt. hp.: 94.88
Max. available drawbar hp.: 83.79
Specific fuel consumption hp.-hrs./gal.: 15.82
Weight as tested (lbs.): 14,265
Engine disp./trans.: 404/SR

Model 4020 LPG
Test Number 934
Date: 4-1966
Max. belt. hp.: 94.57
Max. available drawbar hp.: 83.59
Specific fuel consumption hp.-hrs./gal.: 9.24
Weight as tested (lbs.): 14,150
Engine disp./trans.: 340/SR

Model 4020 Gas
Test Number 939
Date: 5-1966
Max. belt. hp.: 95.59
Max. available drawbar hp.: 83.28
Specific fuel consumption hp.-hrs./gal.: 12.12
Weight as tested (lbs.): 14,030
Engine disp./trans.: 340/SR

Model 4020 Gas
Test Number 1012
Date: 6-1969
Max. belt. hp.: 95.66
Max. available drawbar hp.: 82.57
Specific fuel consumption hp.-hrs./gal.: 10.3
Weight as tested (lbs.): 13,820
Engine disp./trans.: 362/PS

Model 4020 Gas
Test Number 1013
Date: 5-1969
Max. belt. hp.: 96.66
Max. available drawbar hp.: 84.52
Specific fuel consumption hp.-hrs./gal.: 11.71
Weight as tested (lbs.): 13,800
Engine disp./trans.: 362/SR

Model 4020 Diesel
Test Number 1024
Date: 9-1969
Max. belt. hp.: 95.83
Max. available drawbar hp.: 83.09
Specific fuel consumption hp.-hrs./gal.: 14.77
Weight as tested (lbs.): 13,980
Engine disp./trans.: 404/PS

Production Totals

Type	Fuel	Number Built
Row Crop	Gasoline	3,613
	LPG	4,459
	Diesel	36,736
Standard	Gasoline	98
	LPG	792
	Diesel	11,370
High Crop	Gasoline	*
	LPG	17
	Diesel	170
Industrial		
	Gasoline	10
	Diesel	170
Special Standard **	Diesel	36

*One built and shipped, but later returned and converted to diesel.

**Export only

Model 4020 Serial Number vs. Year Model

Year	Beginning Serial Number
1964	65000
1965	91000
1966	119000
1967	145660
1968	173892
1969	201000
1970	222143
1971	250000
1972	260791

This 1972 Model 4020 with dual hydraulics and a three-point hitch, is earning its keep every day. It is standing in front of a 1962 Ford pickup, also still at work.
Owner: Arvin Brusenitz

Model 4000

The competition between Deere and International Harvester was at a fever pitch at the end of the decade of the '60s. Deere kept one step ahead with the Twenty-Series, but Harvester proved to be a nimble and capable competitor, offering a variety of good-performing, smooth-running six-cylinder tractors in the over-75-horsepower class. The I-H Torque Amplifier effectively gave their tractors more available ratios than those of Deere. The Deere 3020 and 4020 were certainly able to carry the fight to the enemy, but there was a significant horsepower opening between them. The four-cylinder 3020 was at 65 hp in 1963 and the six-cylinder 4020 was at 91 hp. The six-cylinder Farmall 756 engine produced 72 hp in its Nebraska test, while the 856 was at 95 hp. The Deere tractors were competitive, but the I-H offerings had the advantage. Besides, the new Deere multi-cylinder engines were no match for the old two-cylinder diesels in specific fuel consumption, nor did they match the I-H offerings in that area.

By 1966, Deere had upgraded the 3020 to 76 hp, and the 4020 to 96 hp by the end of 1967. The 1966 Nebraska tests of the Farmall 756 and 856 revealed horsepowers of 76 and 100 respectively. For 1967, I-H added hydrostatic transmissions for smooth, stepless shifting.

The marketing people at Deere recognized two of the most important factors farmers considered in choosing a new tractor were horsepower and price. The Deere offerings were more refined and had better service records, but the horsepower-per-dollar factor

In the late 1960s, Deere decided to fill the gap between the 3020 and the 4020 with the new Model 4000. Essentially a bare bones 4020, it had 4010-sized final drives. Produced 1969 to 1972, this 1971 is a 4000 Low-Profile, one of only 46 made. Owner: Keller Collection

was swinging sales to I-H. Someone at Deere, probably a recruit from the automobile industry, came up with the idea of "hot-rodding" a tractor. In other words, they put a big engine in a lighter tractor, and also removed all non-functional frills to get the price down.

Technically, the idea had merit. The same implements could be worked faster, thereby getting more done per day. The danger was if larger implements were worked at the same speed as before, the lighter drive train could be in trouble. In checking the over-strength of the 4010 final drive, it was decided the risk was worth it, and the Model 4000 was born. It was essentially a 4010 with a 4020 engine. While that is perhaps an over simplification, the result was a tractor 1,000 lbs. lighter and $1,000 cheaper. To achieve the weight and price goals, there were changes to the 4000 from the 4010 and the 4020. All the ergonomic features were retained, but battery boxes were eliminated. Only one headlight graced the flat-top fender instead of two. A single hydraulic system and a 540 rpm-only PTO were standard, as was a lighter 3-point hitch. The Syncro-Range transmission did not have the synchronized reverse and panel lighting was down to one bulb. Many of the 4020 features could be added at extra cost, but there was little point in building the 4000 up to the same price as a 4020.

For the 1970 model year, the available option list was expanded to include such features as longer axles and a gasoline engine. In 1971, the option of the Power Shift transmission was added, and in 1972, the last year for the 4000, almost everything available for the 4020 could be ordered for your 4000 including an air-conditioned cab.

The big change for 1972 was the offering of the Model 4000 Low-Profile. The L-P was four inches lower at the hood line; it had a lower seat and steering wheel and smaller diameter wheels. The front axle, the same as that used on the 3020 row-crop utility was mounted farther back on the frame for a shorter turning radius. For the first time, fruit growers and others with the need for a low silhouette, low center of gravity, agile tractor, could get one with nearly 100 horsepower.

While the L-P tractor was a good idea, only 46 were sold. Only 255 of the gasoline versions were sold to farmers more concerned with cold-weather starting than with power and fuel economy (it used the 340 cid, 88 hp six from the 4020). The 4000 High-Crop version is extremely rare. Only three were shipped, all with diesel engines and all in 1969, to Northfield, Minnesota.

Model 4000
Data and Specifications

Overall years built: 1969-1972
Built at: Waterloo, Iowa

Available configurations:
Row crop (gasoline, diesel)
Low-profile (gasoline, diesel) (only diesels built)
High crop (diesel) (only 3 built)

Wheels/Tires:
Row Crop Tractors
    Front: 6.00-16, 7.50-15, 9.5L-15 (adjustable
      –wide)
    Rear: 13.6, 14.9, or 15.5-38; 16.9, or 18.4-34;
      18-4-30
    Power adjustable rear wheels: 34 or 38-inch
      wheels
High Crop Tractors
    Front: 7.50-15
    Rear: 15.5-38
Low-profileTractors (available 1973 model year)
    Front: 9.5L-15
    Rear: 18.4-30, 18.4--26

Wheelbase: 96 inches (row-crop)

Engine Options:
Gasoline*
    Number of Cylinders: 6
    Bore & Stroke: 4.25 x 4.25 in.
    Displacement: 360 cid
    Rated RPM: 2200
    Cooling: Pump
    Compression Ratio: 7.5:1
Diesel
    Number of Cylinders: 6
    Bore & Stroke: 4.24 x 4.75 in.
    Displacement: 404 cid
    Rated RPM: 2200
    Cooling: Pump
    Compression Ratio: 16.5:1
*Gasoline engine optional in 1971

Transmission:
Synchro-Range, eight-speed (four-speeds with two-range auxiliary).
Travel speeds from 1.8 mph to 16.8 mph.
Power-Shift optional in 1971.
Two reverse speeds.

Electrical: 12-volt (alternator)

Shipping weight: 7,670 lbs.

Price, new: $5,000, diesel row crop

4000 production totals

7,987 built

| | Diesel | | Gasoline | |
	Syncro-Range	Power Shift	Syncro-Range	Power Shift
1969	1,799	N/A	N/A	N/A
1970	1,849	N/A	90	N/A
1971	2,011	156	124	5
1972	1,635*	272**	42	4
Total	7,294	428	256	9

*   21 were Low-Profile

** 25 were Low-Profile

Nebraska Test Data
Model 4000
Test Number 1023
Date: 10-1969
Max. belt. hp.: 96.89
Max. available drawbar hp.: 85.29
Specific fuel consumption hp.-hrs./gal.: 15.65
Weight as tested (lbs.): 10,870

Model 4000 Serial Number vs. Year Model

Year	First-Last Serial Numbers
1969	211422-222202
1970	222267-242303
1971	250014-260786
1972	260797-270280

In 1971, Deere again found itself with a power gap between its 4620 at 135 horsepower and its 4020 at just under 100. Archrival Harvester had turbocharged its Model 806, making it into the Model 1206 in 1965. The 1206 (upgraded to the 1256 in 1968), developed about 115 horsepower and Deere had nothing like it to offer. The 5020 Row Crop of 1967 was Deere's first attempt at an over-100 horsepower row crop tractor. It was deemed to be too cumbersome by customers and was replaced by the Model 4520 and then the 4620, but the power gap remained. Taking a page from its competitor's design book, Deere then added a turbocharger to the already-beefy 4020 engine, redesigned and strengthened the drive train, adding almost 700 lbs. The result was a 115 hp Super 4020. It was designated the Model 4320.

The 4320 was much the same as the 4020 in size and shape. All of the 4020 features were extended to the new model. The new 4320 was, however, offered only in the row crop configuration and only with the Synchro-Range transmission. Front end options included the adjustable wide front, dual tricycle (with or without Roll-O-Matic), single front wheel, and hydraulic FWA (Front Wheel Assist). A fixed-tread front axle was also available, as were other optional features that would essentially make the 4320 into a standard-tread tractor.

The three-point hitch was standard, but could be deleted in favor of a swinging drawbar. One remote hydraulic outlet was standard, but two more could be added. The standard PTO setup accommodated both 540 and 1000 RPM implements, but the whole PTO, or just the 540 option, could be deleted to reduce the price. The Roll-Gard ROPS, or the Roll-Gard with canopy could be added. A factory cab was also available.

Front end options included the adjustable wide front (fixed or adjustable), dual tricycle (with or without Roll-O-Matic), single front wheel, and hydraulic FWA (Front Wheel Assist).
Owner: Keller Collection

A 1972 version is shown with FWA, a Roll-Gard and canopy.
Owner: Keller Collection

The three-point hitch was standard. The 4320 was offered in 1971 and 1972.
Owner: Keller Collection

Model 4320
Data and Specifications

Overall years built: 1971-1972
Built at: Waterloo, Iowa
Available configurations:
Row Crop

Wheels/tires:
Front: 10.00-16, 7.50-15, 11L-15 (adjustable–
wide, single front wheel, or dual tricycle
with Roll-O-Matic optional).
Hydraulic Front Wheel Assist, optional
Rear: 18.4, 20.8-34; 15.5, 16.9, 18.4-38; 23.1-30
(single)
13.6, 15.5, 16.9, 18.4-38; 18.4-34 (dual)\

Axles:
Standard – 60 to 91 inches
Long – 67 to 105 inches
Extra long – 66 to 115 inches

Wheelbase: 96 inches

Engine options:
Diesel
Number of Cylinders: 6
Bore & Stroke: 4.24 x 4.75 inches
Displacement: 404 cid
Rated RPM: 2200
Cooling: Pump
Compression Ratio: 15.7:1
Turbocharged

Transmission:
Synchro-Range: eight-speed , 2-speed reverse
Travel speeds from 2.0 mph to 18.9 mph

PTO: 540 and 1000 rpm (live)

Shipping weight: 9,050 lbs

Price, new: $10,000 (1971)

Nebraska Test Data
Model 4320
Test Number 1050
Date: 9-1970
Max. belt. hp.: 116.6
Max. available drawbar hp.: 101.7
Specific fuel consumption hp.-hrs./gal.: 14.65
Weight as tested (lbs.): 14,380

Model 4320 Serial Number vs. Year Model
Year	First Serial Numbers
1971	6000
1972	17031

Horsepower is a measure of the rate of doing work, while torque is a force that can be applied with, or without movement. The fact that the Deere two-cylinder engines had such good lugging ability was because of their capacity to generate bags of torque while turning near their rated RPM and then holding it as the RPMs fell off. The horsepower of even the greatest two-cylinder, that of the 830, was less than 75. Never mind it could lean into a load until something broke, it was limited in the amount of work it could do in a day to that which could be accomplished with 75 horsepower. Some western farmers substituted GM 2-cycle blown 6-71 engines, with almost twice the horsepower, in their John Deere 830s. They got almost twice the amount of plowing, or tilling, done in the same length of day, in spite of the fact the torque of the GM engine falls off rapidly if the engine is lugged below its normal howling point. The extra load on the final drive and clutch made for greatly foreshortened lives, however.

So, how else could a western wheat farmer get more work done per day? One way was to buy two JD 830s, and many did, but that required a hired operator. One put two 830s in tandem so that one could drive both. Another thing that could be done was to complain to

The big Deere Model 5010 used an eight-speed Synchro-Range transmission. Shipments began in August 1962 with the 5010 listed as a 1963 model.
Owner: Arvin Busenitz, Newton, Kansas

your dealer that you wanted more horsepower, and lots of it, and many farmers did that, too.

In the far west, some had turned to crawlers, which by the mid 1950s had become capable of utilizing 150 hp diesel engines. These worked well enough, especially where steep side hill situations were present, but they were expensive to buy, expensive to maintain, and since they were relatively slow, they required huge implements to absorb the horsepower.

The horsepower of wheel tractors had peaked in the post World-War II era at about 50. Strangely, the most powerful tractor one could buy in 1950 was the Funk conversion of the 8N Ford. A man named Delbert Heusinkveld installed a Ford 8BA industrial engine in his 8N and handily won a terracing contest against all comers. The engine was rated at 100 horsepower, but at the RPM appropriate for the tractor, it made about 85. The Funk Brothers, foundrymen from Coffeeville, Kansas, took up the cause and began converting Fords, new and used, to Ford V-8 or six power. They did this for several years until their factory burned down. The Funk Brothers continued as foundrymen (and aircraft builders) until, many years later, they were finally bought out by none other than Deere Incorporated.

Meanwhile, production wheel tractors eventually got up to about 75 horsepower, and the farmers complaints finally reached the right ears at John Deere.

By 1953, the decision had been made to go ahead with the New Generation tractors. Three sizes were planned for the Waterloo operation to build: 60, 80 and 100 hp. Development continued to 1960 when the smaller two of the three were introduced as the 3010 and the 4010. The larger 5010 would require more development and didn't come out until the 1963 model year.

All but the smallest of the New Generation tractors got the new 8-speed Synchro-Range transmission, instead of the 5-speed units of the two-cylinder tractors. While the New Generation four and six-cylinder engines had excellent torque curves, they couldn't lug like the two-cylinders. More gears were necessary to multiply the engine's torque.

When the development of the 5010 progressed to the field stage, it was found that current tires were not adequate for the horsepower (which was coming in at around 120 hp). New tires were made by the tire companies in the 24.5-32 size. Long axles were available for those wanting to use smaller dual tires. Specialized rice tires and rice equipment were also available, but the "Rice Special" decal was not used on the 5010.

PTO shafts could not reliably handle the torque at 540 RPM, so the 5010 was provided only with a 1000 rpm PTO. Other options included a three-point hitch and a cab. A variety of heavy-duty implements were developed by Deere for the power of the 5010.

The John Deere Model 5010 was produced from August 1962 through the 1965 model year. This one is missing a right side panel Owner: Arvin Busenitz, Newton, Kansas

Model 5010
Data and Specifications

Overall Years Built: 1963-1965
Built at: Waterloo, Iowa

Available configurations:
Standard Tread – (Wheatland, or Rice)

Wheels/tires:
Front: 11.00-16
Rear: 24.5-32 (single), 18.4-34 (single or duals)

Engine:
Inline Six-cylinder Diesel, Overhead Valve,
Four-cycle
Bore & Stroke: 4.75 x 5.00 inches
Displacement: 531.6 cid
Rated RPM: 2200 rpm (2500 rpm with foot
throttle governor override)
Compression Ratio: 16:1
Cooling: Thermostat and pump

Starter: 24-volt direct electric starting, four 6-volt
batteries (other electrical functions, 12-volts)

Transmission: Deere Synchro-Range, 8-speeds
fwd, 3-reverse
Travel speeds 1.75 to 20mph (with foot-throttle
governor override.

Shipping weight: 12,925 lbs. with standard
equipment

Price, new: $10,730 with standard equipment

Nebraska Test Data
Model 5010
Test Number 828
Date: 10-1962
Max. belt. hp.: 121.12
Max. available drawbar hp.: 105.92
Specific fuel consumption hp.-hrs./gal.: 15.03
Weight as tested (lbs.): 17,175

Model 5010 Serial Number vs. Year Model

Year	First and Last Serial Numbers
1963	1000-4500
1964	4501-7999
1965	8000-10681

Note: All serial numbers in sequence not used. Industrial version also in sequence. Estimated total number of agricultural 5010s is 5,438.

Deere's first two-wheel drive tractor with over 100 hp, the big 5010 used a 531-cid six-cylinder engine. It was offered as a diesel standard-tread, only.
Owner: Arvin Busenitz, Newton, Kansas

Model 5020

As powerful as the Model 5010 was, users contended that it could use even more power. Because the tractor was so heavy (working weight was about 17,000 lbs.), it consumed a lot of its own horsepower just carrying itself around. When the New Generation line was upgraded in 1966, engineers at Deere found a way to coax about 10 percent more horsepower from the engine of the new Model 5020. This was done without changing engine speed, displacement, or by resorting to supercharging. What was done was a refinement of the combustion chambers, injectors were improved and the compression ratio was slightly increase. The results were encouraging, so in 1969, more was done to improve the power. This time, the increase of ten more horses was mostly obtained by turning up the injectors. Nevertheless, the 5020 was now in the 140 horsepower class.

The only transmission offered for the Model 5020 was the eight-speed Synchro-Range unit. It offered four main gear ratios with high and low in each gear. The three lowest ratios also offered a reverse. Thus, one could shift readily between forward and reverse in each of those gears, which was handy for loader operation.

For the 1967 model year, Deere launched the 5020 Row Crop version. It was different from the Standard in that it had swept-back front axles which shortened the wheel base (to improve maneuverability), and longer king pins (after the fashion of the utility tractor) to give the front axle about 3 more inches of crop clearance. The front axle was adjustable from 64 to 81 inches in one version, and from 71 to 88 inches in another. Row-crop fenders and "cockpit" shields were also included.

The 5020 was comfortably equipped with instrumentation, lights, steps, adjustable seat, power steering, power brakes, and a hydraulic system, but a long list of options was available to tailor the tractor to its intended use. The options list included:

- Cab with heater (A/C available in 1971).
- Roll-Gard ROPS (with, or without sun shield).
- Live 1000rpm PTO.
- Three-point hitch with Quik-Coupler.
- Remote hydraulics, dual or single.
- Power differential lock.
- Long/extra long rear axles.
- Horn.

Model 5020
Data and Specifications

Overall years built: 1966-1972
Built at: Waterloo, Iowa

Available configurations:
Standard Tread
Row Crop

Wheels and tires:
Front: 11.00/18.4-16, 9.50-20,
Rear: 24.5-32, 14.4/18.4-38 (single or duals)

Engine:
Inline six-cylinder diesel, overhead valve, four-cycle.
Bore & stroke: 4.75 x 5.00 inches
Displacement: 531.6 cid
Rated RPM: 2200 rpm (2500 rpm with foot throttle governor override)
Compression ratio: 16.5:1
Cooling: Thermostat and pump

Starter: 24-volt direct electric starting, four 6-volt batteries.
12-volt direct electric starting, alternator, after S/N 25000.

Transmission:
Deere Synchro-Range, 8-speeds fwd, 3-reverse.
Travel speeds 1.75-20mph (with foot-throttle governor override.

Shipping Weight:
13,560 lbs. Standard
12,355 lbs. Row Crop

Price, New: $14,600 Standard equipment

Nebraska Test Data
Model 5020
Test Number 947
Date: 9-1966
Max. belt. hp.: 133.25
Max. available drawbar hp.: 113.72
Specific fuel consumption hp.-hrs./gal.: 16.21
Weight as tested (lbs.): 21,360

Model 5020
Test Number 1025
Date: 10-1969
Max. belt. hp.: 141.34
Max. available drawbar hp.: 121.86
Specific fuel consumption hp.-hrs./gal.: 15.46
Weight as tested (lbs.): 19,630

Model 5020 Serial Number vs. Year Model

Year	First and Last Serial Numbers
1966	12000-15559
1967	15560-20398
1968	20399-24038
1969	24039-26623
1970	26624-30002
1971	30003-30612
1972	30613-31130

Note: All serial numbers in the sequence not used. Industrial versions also in the sequence. Serial Numbers listed do not include the prefix T323R-0 for Standard versions and T313R-0 for Row Crops. All had an R at the end of the S/N. Example: T313R-031130R, S/N of last 5020 shipped. The Standard designator prefix was dropped in January 1969 (@ S/N 25000). After that, all used the T313R designator.

Model 4520

Turbochargers – not a new concept in 1969, even for farm tractors, but one Deere resisted for a time. Allis-Chalmers was first to use a turbocharger on their 1961 Model D-19. International Harvester had begun turbocharger use with their 817 cid Model 4300 diesel in the same year (the 4300 was Harvester's answer to Deere's 8010). What caused Deere engineers to rethink their objections to turbocharging was Harvester's Model 1206, which came out in 1965. The 1206 was essentially a Model 806 (comparable to the Deere 4020) turbocharged to 112 PTO horsepower. The I-H Model 1206 neatly filled the gap between the Deere 4020 at 91 horsepower and 5020 at 133 horsepower.

No one disputed the fact that turbochargers were good things for aircraft. There was, and still is, a school of thought that for ground use, naturally-aspirated engines were the way to go. If more power was needed, simply increase the displacement. In essence, that is what a supercharger does (either a turbocharger, or an engine-driven compressor). A larger volume of air is packed into the cylinder and more fuel can be added. For gasoline engines, or their equivalent, where power is controlled by an intake throttle, it can be easily seen that the turbocharger works against the throttle. Unless the throttle is wide open, the turbocharger is just excess parts. On a diesel, where power is controlled by fuel flow, and there is no inlet air throttle. The turbocharger causes the engine to run even leaner at low loads, and to put out even more power when more is called for.

As a stop gap measure, Deere configured a row-

The Model 4520 platform could be open with only the Roll-Gard ROPS (Roll-Over Protection System) or Roll-Gard with canopy. Heater and/or air conditioning were options. This 1969 version has the Power Shift, and no FWA or ROPS. It doesn't have the troublesome air cleaner system of the early 4520s.

crop version of the 5020, providing a little more crop clearance. The 5020 still had the image of a big lumbering standard, and not too many farmers went for it. The M&W Gear Company was offering turbocharging kits for the 4010 and 4020 with considerable success. Deere engineers were becoming convinced that turbochargers did make sense for diesel tractors where row-crop nimbleness precluded high-displacement engines. Also, recovery of the energy wasted in the exhaust resulted in slightly better horsepower-hours per gallon of fuel.

A turbocharger consists of a centrifugal compressor on one end of a shaft with a radial inflow turbine on the other. Exhaust gas from the engine cylinders drives the turbine to high speed. The turbine drives the compressor via the common shaft. The compressor forces air into the intake manifold at two to three times atmospheric pressure. The harder the engine works, the more power there is in the exhaust to drive the compressor, which

gives the engine more power to pull the load. Unlike plain superchargers, such as are used in the GM 2-cycle diesels, the turbocharger consumes only power that would otherwise have been wasted in the exhaust.

In 1909, a Swiss engineer named Dr. Alfred J. Buchi invented the turbocharger. Nothing much came of it until World War II. General Electric had experience with water and steam turbines for driving generators and made turbochargers for most of the high-performance U.S. military aircraft, allowing the engines to retain their power as they went to higher altitudes. Most first line U.S. aircraft in World War II used GE turbochargers. This technology also resulted in General Electric becoming one of three or four preeminent jet engine manufacturers today.

Simply adding a "turbo" to an existing engine is effective, but fraught with danger. While Deere started with the 4020's basic 404 cid engine, both it and the drive line were substantially redesigned. Lubrication, cooling, transmission, brakes, rockshaft, hydraulics, and hitch parts were all "Turbo Built," as advertising of the day stated. Either a SyncroRange transmission, or power shift unit could be ordered for the 4520. Many transmission and final drive parts were similar in size and strength to those of the 5020.

The 4520 was new in other areas, as well. The platform could be open with only the Roll-Gard ROPS (Roll-Over Protection System), could be a Roll-Gard with canopy, or enclosed with a Roll-Gard cab. Heater and/or air conditioning were options. Only a 1000 rpm PTO was offered. Later, hydrostatic FWA (Front Wheel Assist) was added to the option lineup.

One of Deere's bragging points, the air cleaning system, was also the tractor's "Achilles Heel." Rather than the conventional upright air stack with precleaner, an under-hood dual canister system was devised. Air entered through 12 swirl tubes that separated heavy particles by centrifugal force. A venturi in the muffler

sucked these particles into the exhaust, which carried them overboard. The intake air, with about 90 percent of the dirt removed by the swirl chambers, proceeded through the dual dry canister filters before going into the compressor and engine.

In service, this system began to experience failures in such a way that dirt was dumped into the engine. In some cases, the dry filters even caught fire and were sucked through the compressor into the engine. The result was catastrophic engine failure in short order, and unhappy customers. What happened was similar to the fiasco that Harvester ran into with driveline failures on their models 460 and 560 in 1958.

Deere and International Harvester had a similar response. To placate unhappy customers, Deere paid for updates and fixes, including new engines at much reduced costs, long after warrantee periods had expired. Once the air cleaner problem (and a problem with its fuel injectors) was solved, the tractor went on to farm in the true John Deere tradition.

The 4520 was Deere's first turbocharged tractor. They started with the basic 404-cid 4020 engine, but both it and the driveline were substantially beefed up.

Model 4520
Data and Specifications

Overall years built: 1969-1970
Built at: Waterloo, Iowa

Available configurations:
    Row crop
    Standard

Wheels/Tires:
    Row Crop and Standard Tread Tractors
    Front: 10.00-16, 11.00-16, 9.50-20, or 14L-16A
    Rear: 24.5-32, 18.4-38, 20.8-38, and 18.4-38 or
       12.4-42 duals

Wheelbase: 106 inches

Engine:
Diesel
    Number of Cylinders: 6
    Bore & Stroke: 4.25 x 4.75 inches
    Displacement: 404 cid, turbocharged
    Rated RPM: 2200
    Cooling: Pump, 100 gpm
    Compression Ratio: 16.0:1

Transmission:
    Synchro-Range, eight-speeds forward
    Travel speeds from 1.95 mph to 18.3 mph.
    PowerShift, eight speeds forward.
    Travel speeds from 1.72 mph to 18.47 mph.

Three-Point Hitch: Category 2 or 3

Power Takeoff: 1000 rpm, only

Shipping Weight: 13,100 lbs. to 14,500 lbs.

Price, New: $11,600 - $12,500

Nebraska Test Data
Model 4520
Test Number 1014*
Date: 6-1969
Max. belt. hp.: 122.36
Max. available drawbar hp.: 107.76
Specific fuel consumption hp.-hrs./gal.: 15.08
Weight as tested (lbs.): 17,955

Model 4520
Test Number 1015**
Date: 6-1969
Max. belt. hp.: 123.39
Max. available drawbar hp.: 111.21
Specific fuel consumption hp.-hrs./gal.: 16.05
Weight as tested (lbs.): 17,850

*Power-Shift
**Synchro-Range

Serial Number vs. Year Model

Year	Beginning Serial Number	# with SR Trans.	# with PowerShift
1969	813R01000	4,688	1,302
1970	813R07055	1,540	364
	Last Serial Number	S/N not used	Total Built
1969	813R07054	65	5,990
1970	813R08977	19	1,904
Total Production, Model 4520: 7,894			

Model 4620

By 1971, the competitive situation between Deere and Harvester was, at best, clouded. I-H was in financial trouble with outdated plants, labor unrest and struggling management. Harvester retained the number one position in agricultural equipment until 1958. At that point, the lead was yielded to John Deere. In an interesting aside, the story is told of William Hewitt, related through marriage to the Deere family, who became chairman of the company in 1955. Shortly thereafter, a piece of I-H dealer propaganda came across his desk. The motto on the bottom of the page caught his attention – "Not Content to Be Runner-Up." This made Hewitt wonder if Deere was content to be number two. He concluded that if the company was, he would change it—and he did!

Harvester was not the only competitor challenging Deere in the early '70s. Massey-Ferguson had acquired diesel-maker Perkins and was making a full range of creditable tractors. Ford, which had gotten through its growing pains of the '60s, had the full financial power of the Ford Motor Company behind its research. Ford tractors were getting over 130 hp from a turbocharged 401cid diesel tested in 1969. Allis-Chalmers, Case and Oliver rounded out the list of challengers. Deere was continuing with an eight-speed transmission, while the others were at 16. Harvester was doing remarkably well with its stable of tractors equipped with hydrostatic, continuously-variable transmissions.

The technical problems encountered with the Model 4520 were a competitive setback for Deere. For 1971, that was to be corrected with the new 4620. It was clearly an update, but with the strong message that the problems of the 4520 had been overcome. Besides correcting the 4520's shortcomings, the new 4620 would have about a 10 percent power boost through the use of an intercooler between the turbocharger and the engine air intake.

The intercooler was invented shortly after the turbocharger, since inlet air temperatures were always a problem. Compressing air causes a temperature rise proportional to the compression ratio. That is a main reason why diesel fuel ignites at the top of the compression stroke. Turbocharger air at a 2:1 compression ratio would increase in temperature about 112 degrees F at 100 percent efficiency. A radial compressor, used in a turbocharger, is usually between 70 and 80 percent efficient. That adds another 50 to 60 degrees. On a 100 degree Kansas summer day, with a turbocharged tractor really leaning into the harness, air entering the cylinders could be as high as 270 degrees. That limits the amount of injectable fuel. The intercooler, an air-to-liquid heat exchanger, drops the temperature dramatically, so full power can be developed.

Because the problems with the 4520 had hurt sales, Deere decided to introduce the 4620 a little earlier than the usual late August date. Production actually began in July 1970. Its production life was also terminated somewhat early in 1972 due to the coming of the Generation II tractors.

Standard equipment was similar to that offered for the 4520. New options were available, however, including a Weather-Shield canvass/vinyl cab, hydraulically actuated differential lock, three-point hitch with Category II Quik-Coupler, and/or three remote hydraulic outlets. Also new for the 4620 was a Power Weight-Transfer hitch that gave draft control advantages of mounted equipment to trailed equipment. Hydraulic Front-Wheel Assist (FWA) was another option. It had two power settings, low and high. The low setting was mainly to improve steering. The system could be turned off if not needed.

The Model 4620 was built in 1971 and 1972. Technical problems encountered with the Model 4520 were corrected. The 4620 shown has the optional cab, FWA, and is the first 4620 built with Power Shift.
Owner: Keller Collection

Model 4620
Data and Specifications

Overall years built: 1971-1972
Built at: Waterloo, Iowa

Available configurations:
    Row crop
    Standard

Wheels/Tires:
    Row Crop and Standard Tread Tractors
    Front: 10.00-16, 11.00-16, 9.50-20, or 14L-16A
    Rear: 24.5-32, 18.4-38, 20.8-38, and 18.4-38 or
        12.4-42 duals

Wheelbase: 106 inches

Engine: Diesel
    Number of Cylinders: 6
    Bore & Stroke: 4.25 x 4.75 inches
    Displacement: 404 cid Turbocharged and
        intercooled
    Rated RPM: 2200
    Cooling: Pump, 100 gpm
    Compression Ratio: 16.0:1

Transmission:
    Synchro-Range, eight-speed (four-speeds with
        two-range auxiliary).
    Travel speeds from 1.95 mph to 18.3 mph.
    PowerShift, eight speeds forward.
    Travel speeds from 1.72 mph to 18.47 mph.

Three-Point Hitch: Category 2 or 3

Power takeoff: 1000 rpm, only

Shipping weight: 14,100 lbs. to 15,500 lbs.

Price, new: $13,300 - $15,500

Nebraska Test Data
Model 4620
Test Number 1064*
Date: 5-1971
Max. belt. hp.: 135.62
Max. available drawbar hp.: 110.92
Specific fuel consumption hp.-hrs./gal.: 14.77
Weight as tested (lbs.): 18,585

Model 4520
Test Number 1073**
Date: 6-1971
Max. belt. hp.: 135.76
Max. available drawbar hp.: 115.75
Specific fuel consumption hp.-hrs./gal.: 14.70
Weight as tested (lbs.): 18,640

*Power-Shift
**Synchro-Range

Serial Number vs. Year Model

Year	Beginning Serial Number	# with SR Trans.	# with PowerShift
1971	10001	2,766	890
1972	13693	2,279	993
	Last Serial Number	**S/N not used**	**Total Built**
1971	13692	36	3,656
1972	16967	3	3,272

Total Production, Model 4620: 6,928

The new 4620 would have about a 10 percent boost in power through the use of an intercooler between the turbocharger and the engine air intake. The 4620, introduced in late August 1970, was terminated in 1972 for the Generation II tractors. Owner: Keller Collection

Articulated four-wheel-drive tractors were almost unheard of until 1959. The first, the Wagner TR-14A was tested at the University of Nebraska in June of that year. The TR-14A was a descendant of the earlier TR-9 non-articulated machine. The John Deere 8010 was also introduced in 1959, along with the Wagner TR-14A, both articulated four-wheel-drive farm tractors. Other manufacturers continued with four-wheel steer types for a while. These big, heavy powerful movers stemmed originally from aircraft tugs. Companies like Hough, Coleman, Clark, Michigan and others had been the providers.

At about the same time as the aircraft tugs, articulated wheel loaders came on the scene. A Company named "Scoopmobile" in 1952 made the first. Not many of these were delivered until later in the decade due to problems with the hinge. It is likely this type of loader was related to the two-wheel tractor/scraper developed by LeTourneau in the late '30s, which incorporated hydraulic articulated steering and such a heavy-duty center hinge.

In the 1950s, farmers desperate for horsepower, traction and floatation, but not wanting to go to crawlers, made some combination tractors. Generally, this was done by removing the front wheels from two tractors, and hooking them together in tandem. A center pivot was incorporated and steering was done by a hydraulic cylinder. Most of these were home-made, but the Doe Company in England sold combined Fordson Major diesels as the Doe Dual Drive, or "Triple-D" tractor.

Other than the John Deere 8010, the original articulated four-wheel-drive farm tractors were

A version of the 8-speed Synchro-Range transmission was employed, but a two-speed auxiliary was an option. A three-point hitch and a rear PTO were also options
Owner: Keller Collection

Shown is the first 7020 built. It has rack and pinion adjustable wheel spacing, a cab and 18.4-34 Firestone tires.
Owner: Keller Collection

essentially home-made, as well. When the Steiger brothers of Red Lake Falls, Minnesota, could not buy the tractor they needed in 1957, they set out to make their own from a Euclid earthmover. They eventually sold more than 100 copies. Today, the company is part of CNH Global NV and still at the forefront of big tractors.

Farmers in the 1960s began to complain that these tractors resembled large highway trucks, more than farm tractors. Indeed, the John Deere 8010 and 8020 were equipped with engines, axles and transmissions acquired by Deere from the truck industry. This was the primary factor in establishing the tractor's price (which farmers thought was too high, and over which Deere had little control).

In 1965, Deere Industrial Division moved into the logging industry with three articulated diesel log skidders. Identified as the JD440, JD540 and the JD740, these machines capitalized on Deere's experience with the 8010/20. They were equipped with Deere-built 3, 4, and 6-cylinder engines and Deere-built axles and transmissions. Later in the '60s, the JD860A articulated earthmover was also introduced.

It took Deere until 1966 to sell the remaining 8020s in inventory, so they were reluctant to bring out another articulated design. Steiger and Versatile were

selling their units to the large-acreage farmers of the Great Plains in record numbers. Deere decided to offer versions of the big Wagner machines, the WA-14 at 225 hp and the WA-17 at 270 hp. Neither had any Deere content, except the green and yellow paint, so there was not much in it for the company.

At the end of the decade of the 1960s, Deere product planners and market researchers recognized the current crop of articulated four-wheel-drives was filling a niche much like that of the old standard-tread tractors of the 1940s. They were limited to heavy tillage duties. These market planners opined that what the world of agriculture needed was an "all-purpose" articulated four-wheel-drive tractor. What was needed was a row-crop tractor with adjustable wheel spacing and the ability to do large-acreage planting and cultivating. The specifications for the new John Deere 7020 were established.

In order to capitalize on the economies of scale, the new 7020 was powered by the same turbocharged and intercooled engine as the John Deere 4620 tractor. A version of the 8-speed Synchro-Range transmission was employed, but a two-speed auxiliary was an option. In true row-crop fashion, a three-point hitch and a rear PTO were also options.

Overall years built: 1972-1975

Built at: Waterloo, Iowa

Configuration: Four-wheel-drive, Articulated, Row crop

Wheels/Tires:
- 18.4-34 single or dual
- 23.1-30 single
- 24.5-32 single
- 23.1-30 and 18.4-34 in combination as duals

Wheelbase: 120 inches

Engine:
- Diesel, four-cycle, with overhead valves
- Number of cylinders: 6
- Bore & stroke: 4.25 x 4.75 inches
- Displacement: 404 cid turbocharged and intercooled
- Rated RPM: 2200
- Cooling: Pump, 100 gpm, 32 quart capacity
- Compression ratio: 16.4:1
- Factory horsepower: 146

Transmission:
- Synchro-Range, eight-speeds (with optional two-range auxiliary -16 speeds)
- Travel speeds from 1.99 mph to 21.4 mph

Hydraulics: Variable displacement pump. Closed center system, two remote systems.

Three-Point hitch: Category 3 (optional)

Power takeoff: 1000 rpm (optional)

Shipping weight: 14,600 lbs to 20,000 lbs

Price, new: $21,700 with cab, duals and 3-point hitch

Nebraska Test Data
Model 7020
Test Number 1063
Date: 5-1971
Max. belt. hp.: 146.17
Max. available drawbar hp.: 127.72
Specific fuel consumption hp.-hrs./gal.: 14.28
Weight as tested (lbs.): 18,495

Serial Number vs. Year Model

Year	*Beginning Serial Number
1971	001000
1972	002007
1973	002548
1974	003122
1975	002542-003708

*Prefix 773R
2,586 Model 7020s shipped
002607-002699 not used

The Model 7020 was an "all-purpose" articulated four-wheel drive tractor that could do large-acreage planting and cultivating. It was powered by the same turbocharged and intercooled engine as the John Deere 4620 tractor.
Owner: Keller Collection

Collector Magazines

Two Cylinder
PO Box 430
Grundy Center, IA 50638
319-345-6060
Toll free: 888-782-2582
memberservices@two-cylinder.com

Green Magazine
2652 Davey Rd.
Bee, NE 68314-9132
402-643-6269
www.GreenMagazine.com

The monthly magazine for John Deere enthusiasts.
John Deere TRADITION Magazine
1503 SW 42nd St.
Topeka, KS 66609
The official magazine of the John Deere Collectors
    Center.

Parts

Detwiler Tractor Parts
S3266 State Hwy 13
Spencer, WI 54479
715-659-4252
detwiler@tznet.com
www.detwilertractor.com

David Geyer Fabrication
1251 Rohret Rd. SW
Oxford, IA 52322
319-628-4257
Hoods for all unstyled JD's and the JD 430.
Custom sheet metal fabrication.

The Farmacy
N1878 Hwy 13 S
Medford, WI 54451
715-678-2224 Fax: 715-678-2640
pharmacy@starband.net

H&J Machining
Hwy 200 East
P.O. Box 126
Carrington, ND 58421
701-652-3289
jsimons@daktel.com
Machine shop - heads, blocks, connecting rod work,
    sleeving and crank grinding.

JD Two-Cylinder Tractors
1161 Hwy 7
Troy, KS 66087
twocylinderjack@aol.com

John R. Lair
295 W 6th St
Canby, MN 56220
507-223-5902
Near original fenders for all John Deere A ,B, & G row
    crop tractors.

Johnson Implement
6530 Maple Grove
Cloquet, MN 55720
218-729-7143
www.greenpart.com
New old stock 2-cylinder John Deere tractor parts.

Robert's Farm Equipment & Tractor Parts, Inc.
11377 State Route 177-732
Camden, OH 45311
800-367-8751
Tparts@c.s.com
www.robertstractor.com

Used rebuilt & new replacement parts.

Morgan McDonald Carb and Ignition
1001 Commerce Rd.
Jefferson, GA 30549
706-367-4179
mmcdonald_c_j@yahoo.com
www.mcdcarbign.big step.com

Ritter Repair
15664 Cord 309
Savannah, MO 64485
816-662-4765
2 cylinder John Deere tractor repairs.
Repair, calibrate and test 2 cylinder injection pumps and
    injectors.

Shepard's TwoCylinder Parts
John Shepard
E633-1150 Ave.
Downing, WI 54734
715-265-4988 Fax 715-265-7568
js2cypts@baldwin-telecom.net
www.shepard2cypts.qpg.com
Specialists in John Deere M-MT-40-420-435 tractor
    parts.

Sierren Reproductions
1320 HWY 92
Keota , IA 52248
tesieren@iowatelecom.net

Taylor Equipment Co.
3694 2 Mile Rd.
Sears, MI 49679
231-734-5213
2 Cylinder Diesel Shop
731 Farm Valley Rd.
Conway, MO 65632
417-589-3843 or 417-468-7000
Jd2cyldiesel@parts.net
Rebuild and service all diesel 2-cylinder fuel pumps.
Also inline P-series pumps, high output/performance a
    specialty.

Willson Farms
20552 Old Mansfield Rd.
Fredericktown, OH 43019
740-694-5071

Woods Equip. Co
200 Lothenback Ave
St. Paul, MN 55118
651-450-2104

Recommended John Deere Paint

John Deere's famous Deere Implement Green is
available from DuPont as code 262 in Dulux, Imron
and Centari.

Deere Implement Yellow is DuPont code 263
available in Dulux and Centari.

Deere's modern Construction Yellow is DuPont
code 43007 in Dulux.

Decals

Jorde's Decals
935 Ninth Av. NE
Rochester, MN 55908
507-228-5483
e-mail: decals@jordedecals.com
web: www.jordedecals.com

Steering Wheels/Refinishing

Minn-Kota Repair, Inc.
38893 Co Hwy 12
Ortonville, MN 56278
320-839-3940
320-289-2473
mert@minnkotarepair.com
www.minnkotarepair.com

Tires

M. E. Miller Tire Co.
17386 State Highway 2
Wauseon, OH 43567
419-335-7010
millertire@bright.net
www.millertire.com
Hard-to-find tires in original tread designs. They offer
    a free catalog.

Co-owner Ray Mesecher's Highland Terrier "Tuppins" is shown guarding the 1942 John Deere Model H.
Owners: Ray Mesecher and Marty Brackin, Hazelhurst, Wisconsin